The Amazing Adventures of Oinky Grub

I0167293

Andy Frazier

THE AMAZING ADVENTURES OF OINKY GRUB

© COPYRIGHT 2011 BY ANDY FRAZIER

Published by Chauffour Books
Printed by Lulu Press

First print edition December 2011

Version 1.0

ISBN: 978-1-4709-8514-1

As always, I would like to thank Wendy for her endurance in supporting me as a writer, and her compliance with my constant appeal for solitude.

I also want to thank Anne, Kay and especially Sarah, my three faithful fans, for all their support and encouragement, without which I am may have never got this far.

But most of all, I would like to dedicate this book to my wonderful sister, Sarah, for the sheer determination she has demonstrated in her own recovery.
Andy Frazier

4

1

The sun was up early this summer morning, maybe it just couldn't sleep. Most of the countryside lay still and silent as its orange forehead peeped over the horizon, emblazoning its golden glow over the landscape. *Most* of the countryside lay silent except for a tiny sound out in a brown dusty field.

Oink...

Oinky wasn't a bad pig, not by pig standards anyway. And pigs do have standards, oh yes! This small pig with seven spiteful sisters and nine bruising brothers needed to have standards. Oinky wasn't the smartest pig in the world, in fact *OINK* was the only real sound Oinky could make when he was just a tiny pink sausage-like piglet. Except, we're not allowed to mention the S-word when talking about Oinky, that would be mean.

To say Oinky's Mum was fat would be a bit mean too. Mean but accurate, for she was a sow of extreme proportions. She didn't move about much these days, she was more into lounging around. Lounging and staying cool. Pigs like to be cool.

Oinky wasn't cool, however, he was more sort of tepid as he lay amongst his extensive family in his overcrowded house in his even more overcrowded field. Not that he had been out in the field, not yet anyway. These were his early pig days and an early pig needs to nuzzle and feed and consider his standards. But above all, an early pig needs to *OINK*, and Oinky was pretty good at that.

"Hush!" commanded his mother, "good lord, we're not deaf, do you really have to make so much row this early in the morning?" But he did, Oinky did need to make so much row, because he was little, the very smallest, and he had some making up to do on that day that he came into the world.

The tiny piglets lay in rows, suckling away as their mother slept, with the largest at the front of the queue. That was how it was and that was how it stayed for poor Oinky. He never ever got to the front of the queue and never really grew to be a fine porker like his brother and sisters. Oinky could be more accurately described as a runty-snorter.

* * * * *

"There's no point in keeping that tiny one, it's just taking up space. We may as well get rid of it sooner rather than later," grunted Trotter Edwards to his wife. Trotter Edwards didn't really answer to the name of Trotter; it was just a nickname that the kids at school had given him many years ago. He knew why, of course, it was because of his father. 'Trotter' had been his father's nickname because he had kept a pig farm. But that wasn't the only reason, oh no. You see, Trotter Edwards did bear a slight resemblance to a pig, although he could never see it himself. He was…how should I put this politely? He was man of large girth, he had a shiny fat face, he even had a slightly flat nose and, most significantly, he had a tendency to grunt.

"Well I am not going to deal with it," replied Mrs. Edwards over the breakfast table. The corpulent man just grunted as he tucked into another fine Edwards Pork Sausage and checked the daily pork prices in the newspaper. "It's Barry's birthday tomorrow, we really should get him a present this year," continued the woman, "something nice, you know, something special." The large man still didn't look up from his paper. "He's thirteen this year, you know?"

"Bout time he did some bloomin work then," said Trotter, flecks of sausage-meat spraying over the paper as he folded it up. "Prices like these, I'll be out of business in no time. We could do with some more labour around here. When I was his age I was out on the farm." The door opened and a boy shuffled through it, his red round face glaring out from behind large circular spectacles. The boy said nothing, just made his way to a seat at the table and sat down expectantly.

"I was just saying, bout time you did some blooming work?" said Trotter.

"Now don't start, Thomas, you know Barry doesn't like you to start on him first thing in the morning?" said Mrs. Edwards, piling more sausages on to a plate and putting them in front of the boy. Barry still said nothing, just opened his mouth and pushed two whole sausages in at once and then chewed them noisily. As he shovelled the food in, grease dripped down his chin and onto his stained green t-shirt. The shirt displayed the logo for **Edwards Pork Farm** and had been his birthday present last year. Barry glanced briefly at his father who wore a similar shirt, as did his mother. His two sisters wore them too, and even baby Edward had a tiny one given to him when he was born. Barry thought about the baby. It had been his idea to call him Edward. 'Edward Edwards,' he thought, was quite a nice name and his parents didn't really have much imagination when it came to names.

Upstairs, the floorboards creaked at the old farmhouse and Barry momentarily looked up to the ceiling. That would be Henny and Penny getting the baby dressed, the two girls doing it together. They did everything together, walked, talked even went to the toilet together. Some teachers at school had tried to part them and had even put them in different classes so that they could tell them apart. Sometimes Barry had a job to know which one was which, they were so alike, and they used to tease him about it. Barry wasn't interested in girls. Stupid things they were, always chattering and giggling. Henny and Penny could giggle for hours. If there was a county giggling championship, they would win it, hands down. No, Barry didn't like girls, he was only interested in one thing. Making money!

Barry Edwards had his first paper round when he was ten, from which he saved up all his money to buy a better bike. Soon he decided he didn't really like riding the bike or the early mornings, so, by the age of eleven, he had hatched a plan and had put up a notice at school. *"Delivery operatives wanted!"* it had said, in black felt-tip pen, and two boys had applied. He made a deal to pay them by the hour, minimum wage, and then sent them out to deliver his papers for him. Since then, he had taken on another round as well, by letting the tyres down on Roger Groat's bike every day so he was always late. This round was in the nearby village of Standfinton. Now he had two paper-rounds, with four staff, and the pennies were rolling in before he even got out of bed in the morning. That suited Barry fine as he didn't like getting up in the morning.

Tomorrow was his birthday and the money that his parents would give him would be just enough for him to make his next investment, an ice-cream cart. The ice-cream cart idea had come to Barry last summer when he was standing in a queue for the van in Marley road. If he could get out of school 30 minutes early by missing games, he could grab the cart and push it near the school gates, selling ices to all the kids before the real ice-cream van arrived. It was a genius idea as he even got to eat some of the goodies himself. He hadn't told his parents about his idea, he hadn't even told anyone at school yet, not until the deal had been done. Barry had done all his research and selected his new machine from a website on the internet, the Ice-Kool model. All he needed to do was to plug it into the electric every morning, so that the ice-creams stayed frozen all day, and he had asked permission to do this at the newsagents. It was all arranged.

Barry shovelled in a couple more sausages and then headed back upstairs to his 'office' and set to work designing a poster to put on the school gates.

Edward's Ices
at
Bargain prices

When he had gone, his mother started again. "So what are you going to do with the little one then, if it's too small to take to market?"

"Oh, I dunno, just put in the pot, it will make some broth, or sandwiches, or something," grunted Trotter, not really interested.

"I can't do that!" shrieked Mrs. Edwards, "not while it's alive!"

"Oh, alright, I will stick it for you and bring it in later." The overweight man stood up from the table, wiping his hand across his mouth, as his chair scraped noisily back on the flagstones. He pulled on his wellington boots at the door and stepped outside into the morning sun, selecting a sharp knife from the cabinet in the porch.

2

At two weeks old, Oinky's family had out-grown of the family home altogether. Hutch number 231 was near the bottom of the field, down near the dark wood and, as Oinky hardly ever managed to squeeze in through its little doorway, he spent much of his time down near the fence, rooting in the earth for anything he could find to eat. Twigs, acorns, bits of grass, even the odd worm, made up Oinky's meagre diet these days while his siblings all tucked into his mother's milk. He wasn't really resentful of them, it was just how it was; they were bigger so they got the best seats.

For a short period, he had managed to wriggle his way in to the hut, just once per day. But he would always find himself at the bottom of the pile, with the others all climbing on top of him to get to the milk in their greedy way, as he oinked and oinked in discomfort. After a while, he thought it best if he found his own food, and that was what he was doing now, sniffing out worms. As well as being a very vocal pig, Oinky had an excellent sense of smell, something he found very useful when foraging for food. He could also smell other animals at a distance and he could smell one now, a round human animal in wellington boots, as it sneaked very quietly towards him. Suddenly, a large hand grabbed his tail and pulled hard.

"Come on you little runt, if they were all like you I would be out of business in no time," grunted Trotter Edwards, breathing heavily. Oinky looked into the man's piggy eyes and knew this was not a good place to be, especially when he saw the sunlight glint off the blade in the man's hand. His little mind raced as he tried to pull himself free, when the blade came towards him in an arc. In one last desperate attempt, Oinky managed to turn his head around near enough to his tail to sink his tiny but razor-like teeth into Trotter Edwards' finger, just as the knife was arriving. At first, for a tiny split second, there was silence. Then, the man shouted and released his tail as the sharp blade sliced down. Then, there was blood and squeal. Two squeals, in fact, one of which was coming from Oinky as he and his curly tail parted company. The other squeal came from the large bellied man, whose little finger had joined Oinky's tail, lying on the dirt. They both looked down at the two pink bits of flesh lying on the floor, before the man started to roar.

"Why you little runt..!" he screamed, diving on Oinky once more. But this time Oinky was faster, and was well out of reach, as he raced off across the field towards Hutch number 231, oinking at the top of his voice. His vast mother raised her head to see what the noise was but, when she realised it was Oinky, she just ignored him; that piglet was always making such a row. Oinky tried to squeeze in through the door, so his mother could protect him, but it was no use, the other 16 porkers blocked his path. Worriedly, he looked back towards the man who had attacked him, ready to run again, but Trotter was heading back to the gate with a white handkerchief wrapped around his piggy finger, as he cursed and cursed. Oinky lay down in the shade of the hutch and licked at the stub where his beautiful curly tail had once been, and started to cry.

*　*　*　*　*

12

Barry looked out from his bedroom window to see the blue lights of an ambulance racing up the drive with its sirens blazing. Two men jumped out as it screeched to a halt on the drive, running towards the door of the farmhouse while the dogs barked at their heels.

"Is he still alive?" said the one in the peaked cap, hurriedly, "are we too late? A matter of life and death, that's what the caller said?"

"Of course he's alive," laughed Mrs Edwards, "it's just his little finger. The silly old fool is inclined to exaggerate a bit." Barry thought the ambulance driver looked a bit disappointed when he found out that he hadn't got quite the emergency he was expecting. When the two men went inside, Barry stayed in his room, listening to his father shouting and balling downstairs as though it was his head that had been cut off rather than his little finger. The twins stayed upstairs too, tending to the baby so they didn't have to see the blood. The baby was crying, young Edward did that a lot; he cried for attention, cried for food, cried just because he was crying sometimes. Barry closed the door and continued practising his mother's handwriting on the letter in front of him.

'My son, Barry Edwards, will be off games until further notice, signed Mrs M Edwards.'

It was the signature that he found hardest, she didn't seem to do the same one twice, as he copied it from a couple of old letters that she had written to the council in reply to complaints about the smell of the pigs at Edwards Farm.

When he was happy with the letter, he put it in an envelope and hid it in his drawer along with his other special documents. Then he busied himself with counting his money one more time. Two hundred and seventy one pounds! Barry checked the internet site again to see if the cost price was still the same, three hundred. That meant he just needed twenty nine more pounds to buy his ice cream cart. He scribbled the figure down in his notepad and underlined it. That should be four pounds from tomorrow's paper rounds and twenty five from his parents for his birthday. They had given him that much last year and this year was a special one, he would be a teenager, so maybe they may give him even more? He didn't mind, as long as he got the twenty five so he could complete his investment.

Barry went downstairs to see his father's hand being bandaged up by the medic, as the fat man shouted at them in anger. Without being noticed, he slipped out through the back door, hopped on his bike, as its tyres bulged with complaint, and cycled off down the bumpy drive.

The next morning Barry was up a little bit earlier, the earliest he had been all holiday, in fact, because it was his birthday. He was almost excited about being a teenager; that would make him the oldest in his class, the very first one in form 7A. It wasn't all good though; being a teenager meant he may now have to pay full fair on the bus and at the cinema, but he didn't mind that, because Barry would soon be rich. Scuttling down the stairs, he burst through the door to the kitchen to see his father sitting at the table as usual, but with a white bandage wrapped around his right hand. The twins were down already and Henny was holding the newspaper up for the old man to read, as he searched the column for today's pork prices.

"Happy birthday, Darling!" said his mother from in front of the stove. The two girls both wished him happy birthday too, at exactly the same time, Penny looking up from feeding baby Edward. There were three envelopes in front of his place at the table as he sat down. He ignored the two in the girls' handwriting and pounced on the one marked *Dearest Barry* in his mother's familiar scrawl, ripping the paper away as fast as his greedy hands would go. Inside was a card with a football on it. Why did she always give him cards with football on? He hated football. He glanced at the inscription inside.

To dearest Barry, have a lovely birthday, love from Mum and Dad xx.

Barry's jaw dropped as he turned the card over two or three times, shaking it and then shaking the envelope, while his parents ignored him.

"There is no money!" he shouted, eventually, "you always give me money. Where is my money? I demand some money!"

"Calm down, Dear! This year your father has something special for you. He thinks it's time you became a farmer like he is, and like his father was," said his mother, worriedly.

"But I don't **WANT** to be a smelly farmer. I don't like farming. I just want my money!" The boy's voice shrieked as he shouted because it was just on the verge of breaking. Finally, his father looked up from the newspaper for the first time. "With prices like these, I will be out of business in no time," he muttered, before looking at the boy.

"Well go on then, Thomas," urged his mother, "tell Barry what you have given him for his birthday!"

"What?" said Trotter. "Oh that? Yes, son, I have decided it is time you started a little farm of your own."

"You have bought me a farm?" said the boy looking surprised and greedy, all at once.

"A farm, good grief child, you can't have the farm, you have to work for that. No, you can have…a pig!"

The boy's face went white. What was this, his parents always gave him money? Every year, they couldn't be bothered to buy him a present, so they just gave him some money.

"I don't want a pig," shouted Barry. Baby Edward started crying, spluttering with his milk. Hastily, Penny and Henny looked at each other and then stood up, heading for the safety of upstairs.

"You don't want!?" shouted Trotter, his face going red. "I work my fingers to the bone," he waved his bandaged hand. "My fingers to the bone, so that I can make ends meet. At these prices and all. If I didn't work my fingers to the bone I would soon be out of business. And I offer you a start, a chance to get into the business, and you say you don't want it. You ungrateful little child, expecting everything on a plate!" His mother put a plate of sausages in front of him and the boy grabbed one. "Well," continued his obese father, "you are having a pig for your birthday,

16

whether you like it or not." He tried to pick up the paper again, using the thumb and forefinger on his bandaged hand.

Barry sat devouring his sausages at great speed, fuming about the problem. He needed that money, he needed it to invest, to buy that cart and get it set up before term started again. The boy had got it all worked out and now these silly old people had spoiled his plans. Uninterestedly, he opened the other two cards. One was from Henny, home made, with a car on the front and the other from Penny with a bike on the front. They never bought him presents; they didn't spend their money on him. But Barry didn't mind because it meant that he didn't have to buy them any either, and both of their birthdays were on the same day. That would have crippled his finances.

"What pig?" he asked, eventually. His father ignored him again so his mother spoke on his behalf.

"A really nice friendly young one," she said, "your Father has chosen it specially, haven't you Thomas?"

"What? Oh aye! It's out in the field, you'll have to catch it yourself. Hutch number 231, the one without a tail!"

3

Barry stepped down off his bike and leant it against the gate post. Out in the field, the pigs saw him at the gate and lots of them came running towards him, their ears bouncing as they cantered through the dirt. Hutch number 231 was down near the far wood and the other pigs gathered around Barry when he trudged in that direction. This hutch seemed mighty crowded, as he peered in, looking for one particular one amongst the row of porkers lying down and sucking milk. His eyes scanned the animals, checking their tails, while he pondered the question of why it was this specific pig that his father had given him. Then he stopped suddenly. There, behind the hutch, was the scrawniest looking creature he had ever seen, huddled up against the tin with its tiny ribs showing through its scraggy skin. Barry looked down at Oinky and Oinky looked back up at this fat boy in round spectacles. So that's why, thought the boy, the mean old git has given me the runt of the litter!

Oink, said Oinky. *Oink, Oink, Oink!* The tiny pig sniffed the air and stood up. Oinky was just about half the size of all the others and his little snout twitched sideways when he sniffed. He advanced slowly towards Barry, sniffing all the time, until the boy held out his hand. Oinky cautiously backed away again and hid behind hutch 231. He knew about humans, they had knives, they tried to cut him.

"It's alright," Barry heard himself saying in a baby voice, "it's alright little pig, I won't hurt you." He chucked a couple of cream-cracker biscuits on the ground as he looked at the pig's tail, or the place where Oinky's tale should have been. It was a clean wound and was already healing over. "What on earth am I going to do with a pig?" shouted Barry to nobody in particular, as the pig shovelled the biscuits into his mouth. Oinky looked back at Barry, possibly thinking the same thing.

Then the boy headed back to the gate and climbed on his bike; he needed time to think, he needed time to make a new plan. All he could think was that he just had to have that ice-cream cart, he just *had* to, as he cycled down to the road and on into the village. When he got there he heard the ice-cream van in the distance playing its merry tune. The van was making money in this town, and he wasn't; something had to be done. As very often happens in these situations, the plan came to him out of desperation; desperation and greed.

All of a sudden he knew what to do as he cycled back to the farm as fast as his legs would peddle. As he passed the entrance to the field where the pigs were, he threw down his bike and took out his mobile phone, switching it to camera mode.

*   *   *   *   *

In his room, Barry read through the description he had written one more time, before hitting the upload button.

"Young weanling pig for sale to kind owner. Friendly, happy and house trained, this cute piggy would make a lovely family pet!"

UPLOADING TO EBAY.... said the caption on the screen before it disappeared and the picture of a healthy pink pig appeared in its place.

'Bidding closes by midday tomorrow. Unable to post item, so pig must be collected. Click on the button for any questions.'

Barry smiled to himself as he did a quick search for 'PIG' on E-BAY's main page and the picture appeared at the top of the list. OK, so it wasn't really the same pig in the photograph but it was a similar sort, just a bit bigger. He munched through the rest of the packet of crackers he had taken from the kitchen, while looking at the web page for the Ice-Kool cart again. An email arrived in his inbox and he checked it straight away. It was from ebay, a question.

"What does it eat, from Sarah, aged 8."

Barry thought about this for a few seconds as he looked at the empty packet on his desk. It wouldn't be a lie would it, the pig had liked them?

"C-R-E-A-M C-RA-C-K-E-R-S," he typed and hit the reply button. The message went away and he continued looking at his ice-cream cart until the message box pinged again.

"What is its name?"

"O-I-N-K-Y," typed the boy, smiling to himself once more.

4

Sarah fidgeted in the back seat of the car as they turned off the main road, her mother and father still arguing in the front as her two older brothers sat either side of her looking bored. She had gone on and on to her parents about getting a pet and she knew this one would be perfect, despite what the rest of her family said. The packet of cream crackers lay on her lap, they were made by JACOBS, only the best.

"Slow down, George," snapped Mrs Ryan as the car lurched and bumped up the dusty track to the farm. "Are you sure this is the right place?" Mr Ryan said nothing, just indicated to the electronic navigation device on the dashboard of his new car, as it pictured the track in 3D in front of them. Sarah looked out of the window in amazement as she saw the huge field crammed full of pigs as far as the eye could see. There were large ones, small ones, even a black one that ran along side of the fence following the car, as it approached the farmyard and the big neon sign saying: EDWARDS PORK. A fat boy came towards them as the car pulled to a halt. He was about the same age as her brother Dave, his round face as red as a tomato. The boy took off his large glasses and wiped them on his shirt before putting them back on again and holding out a hand for Mrs Ryan to shake, a greasy smile on his face.

"Welcome to Edward's Farm," he said, in a slightly croaky voice. Sarah's two brothers eyed him suspiciously as he made his way to her. "You must be Sarah?" said the boy,

"I am Barry Edwards." Sarah smiled sweetly at Barry, her ginger curls blowing in the breeze.

"I have brought Oinky some food," she said, "Cream Crackers, his favourite." Barry looked down greedily at the packet in her hand and only just managing to stop himself from licking his lips. Sarah's older brother wandered over to the brick building with the sign over the door marked **Danger, Risk of Electrocution** and tried to look inside but Barry glared at him.

"Dave, don't be so nosey," called out the young girl, as her brother's small diamond earring glinted in the afternoon sun.

"This way, please," said Barry, looking around rather worriedly in case his parents came back. His mother had taken his father down to the hospital to have the bandages changed on his finger and then to do some shopping, but they would be back soon, his knew his father hated shopping nearly as much as he did. "Your new purchase is this way," he continued, striding off down the yard towards the field and undoing the gate, as the family of five town-folk followed him in single file.

"Dun arf whiff?" said Dave to his younger brother when the stepped into the field, "smells like one of yours Kev!"

"Corr! You're not wrong, mate, a real pen-and-ink!" replied Kev. The two boys stepped carefully through the dust, as did Mr and Mrs Ryan, while young Sarah skipped eagerly behind Barry Edwards towards hutch number 231. Before they got there Barry stopped and looked at Mr Ryan.

"Do you have the money?" he asked greedily. "Twenty five pounds I think?" Mr Ryan looked a bit surprised but then pulled out a shiny black wallet from his shiny black trousers and pulled out some notes. Barry couldn't help noticing the man had a huge pile of cash in that wallet. Maybe he should have pushed the bidding up a little bit further, he thought, as he accepted the cash and counted it. "Your purchase is over here," he told the girl, "but you will have to catch it yourself."

The young girl peered into hutch 231 to see the row of porker pigs lying down and suckling at their vast mother. "Aw, they are so cute," she squealed, as they grunted and snuffled. As she did this, one small pink face peered round the corner at them, its snout twitching. "Aw look at the little baby one!"

Barry cleared his throat before speaking. "This," he said, pausing for effect "....is Oinky!" The small pig looked up at him as he spoke, getting ready to run once more, but the girl was rustling at a packet of biscuits with a big smile on her face. She took one out and held it towards the pig while the others looked on. Oinky sniffed at it and then jumped back, so she threw it on the ground near to him and he gobbled it up.

"A bit small, isn't it?" said Mr Ryan, "I thought it would be bigger than that?" Barry looked a bit embarrassed. Oinky was indeed a bit small, approximately half the size of the other ones inside hutch 231.

"Oh, he is much younger than the rest," he lied, "he will grow. He is a very special pig this one. You can always tell the special ones, they have no tails." The Ryan family looked at Oinky and where the missing tail should have been.

"Don't *all* pigs have tails?" said Mrs Ryan, questioningly, but the others ignored her as the young girl offered the pig another biscuit and he took it from her hand. "Grub!" she said softly when the small pig oinked at her, "Grub, Oinky. Yum, yum." She reached down and stroked the pig's bristly head. "Oinky, grub!"

*   *   *   *   *

An hour later, the car pulled into the drive at 17, Manor Gardens with it's windows wide open and, before it had even come to a halt, Kev and Dave jumped out on to the gravel. They were laughing as Mr Ryan complained about the smell; he had been doing that for last half an hour. George Ryan was very proud of his family car, it was the most expensive one in their cul-de-sac and that was important. His conifer hedge was the smartest too, and all the bushes in the garden were trimmed exactly to the same size; exactly, because he had measured them with his tape measure. George was a proud man and it was important to him that he had the tidiest garden in Manor Gardens. So when Sarah's new pet had done a horrible smell as soon as they put the cage in the car, he had been quite upset. He already had a stain on his nice clean trousers where he had fallen in the dirt while they were catching the animal *and* it had tried to bite him as he helped the others get it into the wire cage. But his little girl had been so insistent that she had wanted this new pet and she was his little angel. She would grow out of it, he guessed, like she had done with the dolls house and little pony stories, and at least it was smaller than having a horse. And at least it had stopped squealing.

Oinky oinked happily when the young girl opened the boot to the car and let in some fresh air. He hadn't liked being in that small cage but he did quite like this ginger-haired girl who gave him nice biscuits. Sarah grinned back at him and offered him another one, the last of the packet, which he gobbled down ecstatically while the two older boys lifted the cage out, still laughing about the smell. Oinky wasn't too sure about being lifted out in a cage and started to squeal again, as they carried him around to the back garden, both making oinking sounds themselves and giggling. Sarah instructed them where to put the cage, over in the corner under the weeping willow tree. When she first decided she wanted a pet pig she had done some research from a magazine in the corner shop. Pigs liked shade, it had said, and can eat all sorts of food; that was a plus point. She had told her father that Oinky would be well out of sight under the willow tree, as its leaves and branches hung down like a big yellow umbrella and, she had said, the food costs would be low because he could eat scraps from the house. He would even eat the leaves in autumn, she had told him, in her bid to persuade her father that a pig would make a perfect pet. Eventually, he had agreed, but it was only for a trial period and if it didn't work out, then the pig would have to go. Her father had even asked the fat boy, Barry, if he would have the pig back if they couldn't cope but the boy had said no. In fact, he had said "NO!" very quickly indeed.

Sarah's mum wasn't quite so keen on the idea; she had wanted Sarah to have a pony so they could all join the local Pony Club. In fact, she had wanted her to have the best pony in the district so that Sarah could win rosettes and cups just as she had done as a young girl. Most of all, she had wanted Sarah to win more cups and rosettes that Carol Caruthers's daughter, Imagine, or whatever her name was. That child won everything, just like Carol had done when they were young.

Donna Ryan and Carol Caruthers were very best friends; they had been since they were at school. The two of them went out together shopping and partying, they played golf and tennis; they had even shared a boyfriend at one time in their life. Both had babies around about the same time and both of them had a little bit of surgery done when it was needed. But underneath all the friendship, under the hugs and hello's, there was a little, just a little, hatred. Donna wouldn't have called it hatred, it was more sort of distain. It definitely wasn't envy, oh no, she was not in the slightest bit jealous of Carol Caruthers, with her exceptionally good looks, natural sporting talent, permanent tan and abundant wealth. Not at all! And what about that Mercedes she drove, the one with the fold-down top? Vulgar it was! George would never have one like that, he was far too sensible. But now, after all his years of being sensible and, dare she say, a little bit boring, he had given in to Sarah's pleading and let her have a disgusting pig in the garden. What on earth would *Carol* say about that when she saw it?

Sarah had already made the pen for Oinky and had persuaded her brother Kev to help her. They had used the old kennel that Poppy was forced to live in before her mother had gotten rid of her to a new home. Poppy had been a lovely Spaniel puppy but she kept chewing things and messing on the carpet until eventually her mother had made her live outside in a kennel. But then Poppy had howled and howled for days, hating every minute of being outside and keeping Mr and Mrs Ryan awake, not to mention all the neighbours in Mansion Gardens. There had been complaints and then rows and then complaints about the rows and more rows about the complaints. It had been like those snippets from the Houses of Parliament that Sarah had seen on the TV, everyone shouting at each other, trying to be heard. In the end they had a vote on it and Poppy had lost by 3 votes to two, Sarah and Kev against the other three. Sarah had cried when some people arrived and took Poppy away and she had cried for weeks afterwards too, until eventually her father had agreed to let her have a pet of a different kind.

Oinky stepped out of the cage, sniffing the air and the ground around him. He sniffed a piece of long grass and was just about to eat it when he saw the wooden hutch under the tree, a bit like the one had been born in, only a lot smaller. He not only saw it, he smelt the scent of food coming from it.

"Grub, Oinky!" called out the girl, softly. Oinky broke into a run, oinking constantly until he reached the bowl of biscuits by the tree, after which he only oinked occasionally as he wolfed them down. Sarah stood watching him with delight, her very own pet, her very own pig. With her brother's help, they had constructed a wire fence around the kennel, about 5 metres square, which he could run around in. But, secretly, Sarah knew she wouldn't make Oinky stay in there all the time. When her parents were out, Oinky could have the run of the whole garden, he would be fine as long as she kept an eye on him. She would even take him in the house, because the advert had said he was 'house trained'!

"*Darlings!*" called out a voice, as a woman stepped through the garden gate in her silver and white stilettos and D&G sunglasses. Beside her walked a young girl wearing jodhpurs and riding hat.

"Carol, darling, how lovely to see you!" The two women embraced, offering a fake kiss, "Mwh! Mwh! How *are* you, dear!"

"Oh marvellous, marvellous," gushed the immaculately dressed woman, "Imogen has just qualified for the county trials, isn't that wonderful?"

"Wonderful," echoed Donna Ryan, feigning praise on the girl. Sarah skipped up the garden. "Sarah, say hello to your auntie Carol. Imogen has just qualified for the county what'saname." Sarah said hello and then nodded to Imogen, wondering why the girl was still in her riding hat despite there being no horse to ride within miles.

"I've got a new pet," she said, "would you like to see him?" Imogen nodded solemnly and the two of them went down the garden to see the new pet which was now exploring its new home. Oinky sniffed inside the kennel, it smelled of animal but he wasn't quite sure what sort, and then he snuffled around in the long grass under the willow tree looking for worms.

"Euch!" snubbed Imogen, when she saw Oinky for the first time, "it's a smelly pig!" Oinky looked up at the girl in her riding hat and twitched his nose. This made her laugh. "A pig!" she shouted again, between laughs, "you got a pig as a pet?!" Oinky didn't like this girl who was laughing at him and went inside his kennel, hiding himself under the straw. Sarah looked furious as the girl kept laughing until she could stand it no longer and reached across and pulled Imogen's long plait, which was hanging down under her riding hat. "Ow!" screamed Imogen and pinched Sarah on the arm who then screamed as well. By the time their two mothers arrived, there was a lot of screaming going on and Oinky shivered with fear inside his little kennel. He decided he had didn't like shouting ever since that nasty man cut off his lovely tail.

"Calm down, you two!" said Mrs Ryan. "What on earth is going on?"

"She pinched me!"

"She pulled my hair!"

"She laughed at Oinky!" cried Sarah, through floods of tears, "and now he's hiding!" Sarah went through the little gate and looked into the kennel. Oinky peered out from under the straw with one eye. "It's alright, Oinky, you can come out now," she whispered softly.

"Oh my god!" said Carol Caruthers, predictably, as the small pig emerged from the little hutch and looked at the row of people standing there. "Oh my goddd!" the woman shrieked again. "You have a pig!"

5

Sarah waited patiently until she could no longer hear the sound of the car at the end of the road. Her mother had put her to bed a bit early, as they were going out to a cocktail party, and her two brothers were to keep an eye on her. She could hear loud music coming from their room next door; she knew they wouldn't bother about her for a while and there was at least another hour of daylight left. The young girl jumped out of her bed, pulled on her jeans and t-shirt as quietly as she could and crept downstairs to the kitchen. The leg of the chair scraped a bit too loudly on the floor, as she dragged it towards the work surface, and she froze, hoping her brothers wouldn't hear it. For a whole minute she waited, standing still in case they were listening, but she couldn't hear any movement upstairs, only the thumping of music. Then she climbed on to the worktop and opened the cupboard to where the biscuits were kept, selecting the last packet of cream-crackers, and stepped carefully down again. By the back door she reached up on top of the boiler, feeling around until her fingers found the key to the lock. Sarah always had trouble with the lock on the back door to the garden, you had to raise the handle very hard to get the key to turn and it took all her strength to open it. The evening air was a bit cooler than it had been in the last few hot days, the summer was drawing to an end and there was a threat of rain in the air, as the sun disappeared behind the houses opposite.

Mansion Gardens was in a nice area of Bristol, on the outskirts of the city where there were parks and golf courses. Most of the houses in the cul-de-sac were quite new semi-detached and built of red brick with a garage separating each one. The Ryan's house had a conservatory as well, with coloured glass windows and a row of spikes on the roof that Sarah thought made it look like a porcupine. The garden was quite large and exceptionally well maintained by her father who spent most of his time there, mowing, digging and pruning. The girl made her way down the brick path to the tree at the bottom and its small wire fence.

"Oinky," she called out quietly, checking up to the window upstairs to make sure the boys had the curtains closed. The pig was lying in his little kennel with his nose sticking out, twitching. "Oinky, grub!" she said, unfastening the little gate and going inside. At first the pig jumped up, startled, but then he smelled the biscuits that she held out and was out in a flash, grabbing one and munching it up happily. Sarah stroked his neck as he gobbled it down, his prickly hair rough to her touch. She opened the gate to the rest of the garden. "Come on, Oinky," she said quietly, "are you coming out to play?" Inquisitively, the small pig followed her out through the gate into the garden. Oinky had only ever lived in one place until now and it had been full of other pigs, thousands of them! Now here he was, all alone, in this suburban garden with his new friend and her packet of biscuits.

Oinky had never seen flowers before either, let alone ones growing in rows! He sniffed at a red one and a tiny insect flew out, buzzing noisily. Oinky would have eaten the insect but he wasn't quite quick enough so he sampled the red flower instead. Its petals were quiet sweet and juicy, as he munched it up which his sharp little teeth. Sarah giggled as she watched him investigate the flower bed but then, as

31

he snuffled in the dirt amongst these red flowers, a sharp thorn pricked him on the bum and he squealed out, jumping back as though he had been attacked with a knife. Oinky remembered being attacked by a knife before.

"It's alright, Oinky," said the girl, trying to quieten him, "they are just thorns on the roses," but Oinky was already half-way up the garden, running away from the sharp object before it got him again. He stopped and looked around but could only see the biscuit girl; he didn't think she would attack him, she seemed quite kind. There were some larger bushes in this end of the garden, perfectly round ones with green leaves. Oinky reached up and grabbed one of the leaves but it was quite tough and he had to pull hard to get it. The leaf was attached to a branch which gave a great crack as he pulled it down to his level.

Sarah ran up towards him. "Don't eat that, Daddy will go mad!" she called out. Oinky saw the girl running at him and considered the knife again, before setting off at a gallop towards the house, squealing in panic until he reached the corner and looked at her from behind the shelter of a wheelbarrow. She was calling him again, and offering her biscuits. "Oinky, grub!" she said, keeping her voice low. Now Oinky wasn't the sharpest of animals when it came to intelligence, and he was still very young, but he had good hearing and an excellent nose. 'Grub meant food, and food from this girl meant biscuits, and biscuits were nice.' His snout twitched as he walked slowly back to the girl with the food and accepted the cracker from her hand with an oink. She was whispering to him all the time.

"Oinky, you must not eat the flowers, Daddy will be really upset and he won't let me keep you. And you mustn't...oh dear." Sarah looked down to the pile of pooh on the path. "You mustn't do that either, Mummy is very particular about mess!" Oinky watched her talking as he accepted another biscuit. The girl seemed to smile when she spoke and her eyes were bright and vibrant green. The curls of her golden hair shone in the glow of the last of the evening sun as she looked him in the eye. "You have to behave, Oinky, you must promise me?" The smile disappeared for a few seconds. "You have to behave or Daddy won't let me keep you, do you understand?" Oinky didn't understand at all but he liked the biscuits and oinked quietly. Sarah sat down on a small bench and the pig nuzzled his nose against her leg while she scratched his ear. He liked having his ear scratched, especially by this biscuit girl. Sarah carried on talking to him softly, telling him about Poppy having to live outside in a kennel and about Imogen with her silly horses. The light was starting to fade when she heard a voice calling from upstairs. "Quick!" she said, "you need to get back in your pen." Oinky wasn't sure he wanted to get back in his pen but the girl tempted him with biscuits and he followed her down the path. A light came on over the back door and the voice called out again.

"Sarah, where are you?" It was Dave, her elder brother. She hurriedly tied the string on the gate as soon as Oinky was inside, before running up the garden. "Oh there you are, what are you up to?"

"I was just checking on Oinky, I thought I heard a noise out here," she said, hiding the biscuits behind her back.

"You little monkey," said the boy, snarling at her, "you had better get back into bed before I tell Mum, or she won't be very happy, will she?"

"Oh please don't," said Sarah, looking up at the boy with her big green eyes. She knew he wouldn't, he always threatened her like that. Yes he was nasty to her sometimes and he teased her terribly, but she didn't think he would tell tales. "I am sorry, I won't do it again," she said, and smiled sweetly at him before running in through the door and up the stairs. Sarah knew how to use her smile, she even practised it some days in front of the mirror and she used it at school all the time.

Dave looked briefly around the garden and then went back inside the house. He didn't look far enough down the garden to see a small pig snuffling at the gate that had been closed to keep it in its pen, and he certainly didn't look far enough down the garden to see a small set of teeth chewing through the string that held it shut. The string was no match for Oinky's sharp teeth and it soon gave way. Oinky ate the string, Oinky could eat most things. Then he snuffled under the gate, pushing it with his nose as he cleared up a few biscuit crumbs on the ground. It hadn't really been his intention to escape, he was just after more biscuits and he wanted to find the nice girl who fed them to him. As he went up the lawn he could make out the row of red flowers in the dim light.

6

George Ryan pulled back the curtains in the bathroom at 6am. George Ryan did this every morning at 6am, even on weekends. On weekdays he had to leave for work at 7, to catch the train into town to his job at Davies, Davies and Young. For 4 years, George had worked there as a senior accountant and the pay was good. He was sure he earned more than any of the other men in Mansion Gardens and he had been promised a promotion at the end of the year, possibly even a place on the management board if he was lucky. But today was Sunday and he liked being up early on Sunday so he could get out in his garden, especially as he had spent the day before driving out in the country to buy his daughter a pet. That reminded him, first job was to fumigate the car; Donna had complained all evening about the smell when they had gone to that dreadful cocktail party in town. She had frowned at him too, even kicked him under the table, when he mentioned to her friends that he bought his daughter a cute little pig as a pet. The weather outside was starting to turn, possibly rain today, that would be good, those roses could do with some rain.

George wiped the sleep from his eyes, looked out at the roses, blinked and then looked at them again. Except there weren't any roses to look at, just a row of stalks!

"What the blazes..!?" he shrieked, opening the window to take a better look. A quick scan around his beautiful garden made him sheik even louder. His perfect shaped bushes were no longer perfect, the whole bed of

35

Dahlias were lying flat and...and in the middle of them, was a small pink creature. It was snoring.

"Oi, get out of there!" George shouted out through the window but the animal did not move, in fact it didn't even awake. The angry man pulled on his towelling dressing-gown as he ran down the stairs two at a time, fumbling at the latch on the back door. He pulled on his brown slip-on shoes, hopping on one leg and waving the other in the air as he tried to run at the same time. Oinky woke then, when he saw a man hopping and yelling towards him. He not only woke, but he squealed very loudly, as a man dressed in white approached him waving what was possibly a knife. Immediately, he jumped up and started to run, scrabbling through the mess of flowers around him as he tried to gain grip, still squealing. Dashing towards the corner of the house, he cowered behind the wheelbarrow once more, trailing some rather pretty flowers behind him. George stopped, looked down at what was left his bed of prize dahlias, screamed loudly and then ran at the small pig.

Upstairs, a window opened and Donna poked her head out. "George, what on earth are you making so much noise for? It's barely 6 o'clock!" George Ryan ignored her, focussing only on the creature that had ruined his flowers, the same flowers he was going to enter in Pemberton Flower Show next month. The best dahlias he had even grown, certainly the best ones in Mansion Gardens, now reduced to a pile of green stalks. And what about his beautiful roses? All gone, every one of them! George was not a violent man but this creature would have to be taught a lesson. As he approached the wheelbarrow, Oinky was shaking with fear and oinking very quietly to himself. He tried to make a run for it as the man launched himself in the air, catching the handle of the barrow and sending it crashing to the ground just where Oinky had been. Oinky didn't know where he was running, as he dived through the undergrowth, branches and sticks crashing around him. Suddenly his path was blocked by a brown wooden fence which was much too high for him to even see the top of it. He was trapped. The shouting behind him still continued but it wasn't coming any closer.

"Urrrggh!!" said George Ryan, as he lay on the floor next to the upturned barrow, struggling to breathe. He called out a few more times before other voices replied to him from an upstairs window, all of them telling him the same thing, to be quiet and stop making such a noise. Oinky wanted them to stop making such a noise too and he stuck his head down against the soil in a bid to get away from it. While he was down that low, he happened to notice that there was a slight gap under the fence and snuffled his nose under it. With a bit of pushing and any amount of squeezing, Oinky managed to manoeuvre his little body under the fence and into some similar bushes on the other side. The noise of the shouting had quietened down a little and he felt a bit safer now he was away from the man who may have possibly had a knife. He lay still under the thick bushes, trying to get his breath back, before standing up again and venturing out into the daylight on the other side. As he looked around, he saw he was in a garden, quite similar to the one he had just left, only the grass was a bit longer and there were not so many pretty flowers in it. He sniffed at some yellow ones and ate one, but it tasted bitter and he spat it out. There was still shouting coming from the other side of the fence but Oinky was far enough away to stop shivering and start thinking. Oinky wasn't good at thinking, he was a pig of little brain and that little brain only knew about things like food and survival. Right now he didn't really want food. He had a massive supper the night before, a pack of biscuits and so many flowers he thought he might explode. Oinky had never felt so full, which is why he had just fallen asleep in amongst the patch of flowers.

Something moved in the long grass in front of him and he froze, staring at the moving grass. A black fluffy thin object with a white tip waved above the grass, flapping from side to side. Oinky watched it for a minute or so, sniffing the air. It belonged to an animal and, as he was considering this, the animal it belonged to flew through the air silently towards him. Before he could turn and run it was on his back and sticking sharp spikes into his skin and howling. Oinky ran. Oinky ran as fast as his little legs would go, up to the large house and down a passageway, with the creature still on his back. There was a lot of noise, coming from both creatures, as well as more shouting from an upstairs window. 6.15am that morning was the noisiest 6.15am ever recorded in Mansion Gardens, as more and more people looked out to see what the noise was about.

What they saw was a small and very scared squealing pig running out into the road with a large black and white howling cat on his back, which was now hanging on for dear life. This was a very surprising sight at this, or indeed any other, time of day in Mansion Gardens. The front door opened at number 17 and a young girl ran out wearing a pink dressing gown and matching slippers.

"Get him off, get him off!" she wailed, when she saw the cat attacking Oinky. Through all his fear, Oinky knew this voice as the kind girl who gave him biscuits and screeched to a halt, sending the cat flying forwards. The black and white cat rolled into a ball and then jumped to its feet, its hair sticking up on the top of its back and its tail fluffed up like a feather duster. It looked just as scared as the pig did, when a woman shouted at it from the door of number 15.

"Raffles?" called the middle-aged woman in a red silk nightdress and curlers in her hair. "Raffles, is that you? What are you doing, you naughty cat." She stopped and looked again. "What on earth is that creature?" Oinky looked up at the woman and then at Sarah Ryan.

"It's alright, Oinky," said Sarah, softly, as she approached the trembling pig. Oinky considered running again. It seemed to be the only thing he could do and, what with people attacking him with knives and wild animals jumping on his back, he thought running was the best option now.

* * * * *

Oinky was hiding behind the dustbins at number 7 when he heard the light footsteps and the voice of the girl approaching. He had been there for over an hour and was starting to feel quite safe after his ordeal.

"Oinky, grub Oinky! Oinky grub!" Oinky smelt the scent of cream crackers and couldn't resist a quiet oink as he twitched his nose and shuffled out from behind the big green dustbin. "Oh Oinky, there you are. I was so worried," said the girl, her face smiling as she wiped the tears from her green eyes. "It's alright, Oinky, it's not your fault. Daddy was a bit mad but he has calmed down now." The pig crept forward and accepted the cream cracker, crunching it noisily. "It's OK, he's in here," called out the girl to her brother.

It took the two of them nearly another hour and another whole packet of biscuits before they eventually managed to entice Oinky back to number 17 and into his pen once more. All the time George Ryan was muttering, as he sat in his conservatory pretending to read the paper. He had promised his daughter he would let her have the animal on a trial period and she had now claimed that 12 hours was not a long enough time for him to become acclimatised. That was what had changed his mind, the fact that she had used a word like *acclimatised*, it was a grown up word for a little girl and it had diffused his temper a bit. Then she had used that smile and those green eyes, doing that thing that his mother used to do. And before he knew it, it was him apologising to the blessed pig for scaring it, rather than punishing it for ruining his chances at Pemberton flower show.

Oinky hid inside his little kennel under the willow tree, still shivering from fright. On his first day he had been shouted at, chased and attacked; it wasn't a good start. He licked at the scratches on his back where the wild animal had dug in its claws. It had taken him completely by surprise when it jumped on him for no reason. What if it came back, to finish him off? Oinky wasn't very brave when it came to fighting but he thought he would have to learn if he was to survive in this neighbourhood. He only had two skills, to run fast and to bite. From now on he would have to use one or the other.

Raffles sat on the low wall in the garden of number 15, washing himself in the midday sun. He was still angry about the intruder that had come into his garden. *HIS* garden! He thought all the animals in and around Mansion Gardens knew that number 15 was *his* territory, since he had warned them all off. Raffles didn't have any friends, he didn't need friends, and everyone stayed out of his way. Even that large dog that strutted down the street from Pemberton kept away from Raffles. So what had it been, that pink creature that had arrived through the bushes from nowhere, snuffling about as if it owned the place? Some kind of strange dog, he was pretty sure. He would have to go and find out, and show it who was boss. Raffles jumped up on to the top of the fence and looked over into number 17. He could see the pink animal poking out from the kennel under the willow tree, its nose twitching. The last time he had been in that garden there had been a feeble puppy in the kennel. Raffles had teased it so that it barked and barked until eventually they had got rid of the thing. Perhaps he could do the same with this creature? He certainly wasn't going to let it into his territory again. The cat jumped down from the fence and slunk his way silently around the garden towards the willow tree. When he was near enough to the kennel, he pounced onto the roof and sat there quietly listening. The creature inside was oinking to itself; this should be a doddle. Raffles shuffled up towards the end where the pig was sticking out, and lowered his tail over the edge. All animals were terrified of cats and their tails were their most fearsome part. The tail flapped from side to side, hanging down above the pigs head.

"Hey little animal, I am up here. You better watch your step pal. I am Raffles, King of Mansion Gardens." The kennel started shaking as the little animal inside it got more and more frightened while Raffles sat there smugly swishing his tail. There was nothing in this street that he didn't fear.....was there? But then.

"YEEOOOOWWW!!" screamed the cat, as a pair of razor sharp teeth snapped shut around its tail. The cat tried to pull but the jaws locked tight like a rat trap. Raffles sprung from the top of the kennel landing awkwardly in front of Oinky and went to scratch him. But as he did so the jaws closed even tighter and the pain increased. His wild green eyes glared at the animal, only to see that the small pig had its eyes screwed tightly shut. The pig was making a very loud oinking sound now, as the cat once again gave him a whack with his claw which caught him across the nose. But instead of letting go, the jaws locked tighter still and a sear of pain spread across Raffles as he screamed at the top of his voice. Somebody came running down the garden to see what all the noise was about and Raffles took this as his queue to retreat back to his own garden as fast as he possibly could.

"Oinky?" called Sarah as she saw the blur of a black cat whizzing past her legs, "Oinky, what is going on?" She looked into the kennel to see Oinky, his eyes still tightly closed, clutching a white piece of fur in his teeth. He was shaking uncontrollably.

7

Donna Ryan opened the front door to find her neighbour standing there with her hands on her hips. Donna had never really liked this woman, with her flamboyant clothes and steady stream of male visitors. They had only spoken a few times but the woman never seemed to have anything to smile about. She wasn't smiling now either, as she glared at Donna.

"Mrs Ryan, I have reason to believe you are harbouring a wild animal?" said the woman in a domineering voice. "I caught a glimpse of it this morning and then, this afternoon, my poor little Raffles has been attacked and severely mauled. I am pretty sure it was your wild creature that did it. What do you have to say to that?"

Donna thought fast, as she looked at this aggressive woman. A wild animal? They had a pathetic little pig but it didn't seem very wild to her, quite the reverse, poor thing. It hadn't even got a tail. The poor Raffles she was referring to was that damn nuisance of a cat of hers; Donna had heard her calling it from next door. George had continually chased it away as it kept digging in his precious flower beds.

"What makes you think it is something to do with us?" she asked, defensively. "We don't have any wild creatures, just my daughter's quiet little pet."

"My poor Raffles has had his tail cut off!" snapped the woman, "that does not sound so quiet to me!" Donna thought some more; the cat had lost its tail? Her mind raced, maybe George had put down a trap for the cat and it had cut off the animal's tail? She would need to time to think, time to investigate.

"Well I don't think it is anything to do with us!" she said sharply, closing the door.

"I will report it you know?" shouted the woman from behind the door, "it is an offence to keep a dangerous animal. I will call the police!" Donna's mind raced again. She didn't want the police coming round. What would the other neighbours say? In fact what would they say about a woman standing outside the door shouting *threats* about calling the police. Donna opened the door again.

"Come in Mrs…?" she said, politely. She realised she didn't even know this woman's name. "Come in so we can discuss this. Would you like a cup of tea?"

The two women went through to the kitchen and Donna offered her neighbour a seat at the kitchen table. She was thinking through how to pacify this woman as she unwrapped a fresh packet of tea bags from the cupboard. When Donna opened the pedal-bin to put in the cellophane wrapper she saw the white piece of fur lying amongst the rubbish. Slamming the lid quickly, she turned her back to it in case the woman was looking. "Lost its tail?" she said, her voice going up an octave. Donna was convinced that it must have been one of George's traps that had done this. Maybe that is why he had gone out. He had offered some feeble excuse about going to the pub but she knew he wouldn't, he didn't even drink. No George would be walking around the block, still seething about his beloved garden.

"Yes, poor Raffles. It looks like it has been cut clean off with a knife!"

Donna was convinced now. It must have been George and he had tried to hide the evidence. She would need to protect him. "Well, we do have a small pig," she announced, "it could possibly have been him. He is my daughters little pet, we only got him yesterday!" I will go and ask her.

* * * * *

Sarah heard her mother calling from the house. It surely wasn't bed time yet, so what did she want now? Her mother normally watched her favourite TV program this time on a Sunday. "Coming Mummy!" she replied. Checking that the chain on Oinky's gate was securely fastened, she skipped up the garden towards the house.

"Sarah, this is Mrs....., Mrs?" Sarah's mother looked at the woman.

"Trumpet!" said the middle aged woman, sitting at the table in her flowery patterned blouse. Sarah did her best not to giggle when she heard the woman's name.

"Sarah, this is Mrs Trumpet from next door and she has come to complain about your pet!" said her mother, sternly. Sarah's mind raced. Oinky had been in her garden this morning and she hoped he hadn't eaten all her flowers too.

"I am so sorry he went in your garden!" she said, flashing her big green eyes, "he wont do it again!"

"My garden? Don't be so absurd child," said the woman. "He hasn't been in my garden, not to my knowledge, anyway!"

"So what is the matter then? Oinky hasn't done anything!"

"Oinky?" screeched the woman, "Oinky? What sort of a name is that for a wild animal?"

"He isn't wild, Mrs Trumpet, he is a very timid little pig," said the girl. She had a feeling this wasn't going well.

46

"Timid?" shouted the woman again, "well it wasn't too timid to attack my poor Raffles?"

"I told you that animal wasn't a good idea," said her mother, jumping in on the chance. "I said you should have had a pony, like Imogen. But no, you wanted a wild pig and now look what it has done!" The two women glared at her but the girl stood her ground.

"He is *not* a wild animal," she said defiantly, "he is a poor defenceless little creature. He hasn't attacked anyone!"

"Chopped his tail clean off!" the neighbour was saying, "clean as a whistle. Poor Raffles!" Sarah and her mother looked at each other. Her mother couldn't have known about the tail. She must be bluffing. Sarah's mother had never wanted to have Oinky in the first place and now she would use this as an excuse to get rid of him. And her father had only just agreed to keep him, after a lot of persuasion.

"Well, it wasn't Oinky!" she said again, "Oinky is innocent! He wouldn't hurt a fly!" Sarah could bluff too, even if Oinky had done something bad. She glared at the woman and then at her mother, then stood up and walked back to the garden. Oinky had just about stopped trembling when she opened the gate to his pen. The scratch marks on his face were barely visible after she had applied some anti-septic cream and then covered them with some pink lipstick. She knew he was guilty but she didn't think anyone had any proof.

Oinky saw Donna Ryan and Mrs Trumpet marching down the garden and hid in his kennel. He was already afraid of Sarah's mother but, compared to her, the other woman looked far more fearsome.

"Let me see the wild creature," demanded Mrs Trumpet. Sarah waved a biscuit in front of the kennel and

Oinky poked his snout out just a fraction and twitched it. He looked up at the two women staring down at him. "Oink!" he said, pathetically and then gently took the biscuit from the girl. "You wicked creature," shouted the woman, "you have maimed my poor Raffles for life!"

Donna Ryan joined in as well. She didn't think that it had been this pathetic little animal that had attacked the woman's cat, she was pretty sure it had been her husband who had done that. But she saw it as a way to get rid of the thing before all the neighbours laughed at her and she certainly didn't want the police involved.

"You naughty pig!" she said "first you ruin all of George's flowers and then you attack a lovely defenceless pussy cat!" She looked down at Sarah, with her ginger curls. "Mrs Trumpet, I will personally see to it that we get rid of this animal straight away. Consider the matter dealt with!"

"Mummy, you can't. You can't make me get rid of him. You have no proof. Daddy won't let you. He promised me!" wailed the girl. Donna ignored her and the two women went back up the garden together, talking as though they were old friends, and leaving the girl sobbing. Sarah went and sat by the entrance to the kennel so Oinky poked his nose out and put his head on her lap while Sarah wept for quite some time, stroking Oinky's nose. "They can't make me get rid of you," she kept saying softly. "It's alright, I will protect you. I will look after you!" It was quite a while before she heard her mother and father arguing in the conservatory.

"We can *not* keep that thing!" her mother was shouting, "it will make us a laughing stock!"

"Well I promised Sarah. It wouldn't be fair to go back on my promise," said her father, calmly. The two of them argued for ages, as Sarah strained to listen. It seemed that her father was winning the argument. He told her that the woman next door had no evidence. He also told her that it was not him who cut off the cat's tail.

"Alright," agreed her mother, finally, "another 24 hours!" So that was decided, Oinky could stay as long as he behaved. Sarah lay down beside his kennel and put her arm around him, telling him that he had to be a good boy. Then she kissed his prickly head and went off to bed.

Oinky knew he had done wrong, he wasn't that stupid. But the animal had scared him with its taunting, and it was the same animal that had attacked him earlier. It wasn't as though he meant to bite off its tail, he was just defending himself. He even had the scars to prove it, where the beast had scratched his face. And now he had got the girl in trouble, the same sweet girl who gave him biscuits and smiled all the time. She had even kissed him. Oinky had made up his little mind that he should get away from here before he caused any more trouble.

The next morning the girl came down to see him quite early. "Oinky, grub!" she said softly, opening a large white cardboard box. "We've run out of crackers but I have brought some corn flakes. Do you like corn flakes, Oinky?" Oinky didn't know that he liked corn flakes until he tried them, but he did. He liked them very much, especially when the girl sprinkled some sugar on the top. He oinked quietly as he gobbled them up. While he was busily eating them a car horn blared at the front of the house which made Sarah jump. "Who is that, this time of day?" muttered the girl, making her way up the garden. "Oh, hello Auntie Carol," she said, as she went through the side gate and down the side of the house. "I think Mummy is still in bed." Sarah's mother was indeed still in bed. George had left for work an hour earlier and Donna Ryan never got up too early, she didn't see the point, especially in the school holidays.

Carol Caruthers strode in through the gate and the two of them went in through the back door to the house. "That girl would lose her head," she was saying, "she must have left it here somewhere?" The two of them looked around the kitchen. "She has gone ahead to the gymkhana with her father while I came here to look for her riding crop. Come on Sarah, help me find it, there's a dear!"

Oinky looked out of the open gateway and up towards the house. He took no hesitation in what he did next, and bounded out through the gate, seizing his opportunity to escape. He could see the two people in the kitchen, with their backs turned as he headed silently towards the metal side gate which lead to a concrete path down the side of the house. Out on the front drive was a shiny blue car, its engine still running and the front door open. The inside of the car was very plush, all white shiny leather, as Oinky sniffed at it. Then he heard the back door of the house closing and instantly knew what to do.

8

The sports car accelerated away from the traffic lights as though it was competing in a race. All the while Carol Caruthers was tapping the steering wheel and muttering to herself about being late. She checked the heel of her shoe as she slowed down in yet more traffic, there was an unusual smell in the air today and it seemed to be following her. She liked having the car hood down and checked her makeup in the rear view mirror as a dark haired man smiled at her from a red car in the next queue. Carol secretly liked being admired by other men but, as she was glancing towards this admirer, the car in front of her stopped suddenly and she hit the brakes, screeching the tyres on the dry tarmac. As she did this she thought she heard a faint sound in the back seat. In fact, that was not the first time she had noticed it, it had happened a couple of times. She was convinced it sounded like 'oink'! Carol was just straining around to have a closer look when her mobile phone rang in the handbag on the passenger seat. The woman reached over and grabbed the phone, holding it to her ear and shouting.

"I will be there in a few minutes, the traffic is heavy this morning. I think there's some sort of police hold-up ahead..!"

There was indeed some sort of police hold-up, it was, in fact, a policeman standing in the road in front of her and holding out the palm of his hand.

"Would you pull the car over to the side, Madam?" called the policeman in his peaked cap. Carol pulled a face and then manoeuvred the car to the side of the road. "Great," she muttered to herself. "That's all I need right now!"

"Oh please, officer," she said, turning on a charming smile, "I am running very late. I must get to see my daughter."

"Were you aware it is an offence to use mobile phone whilst driving?" asked the policeman, as he approached the door of the vehicle.

"Oink!" replied a voice from within the car.

"I beg your pardon, Madam?" said the officer, going slightly red.

"I am very sorry," said Carol Caruthers, "I didn't mean it. It was just that my phone rang...."

"Oink," said Oinky, a bit louder now the car had come to a standstill. This time they both heard it and it was followed by a screaming sound coming from the front seat, as Oinky poked his head up from behind it. Carol Caruthers opened the front door of the Mercedes convertible, dived out and started running down the street, much to the dismay of the policeman who believed she was leaving the scene of a crime.

"Get it away from me!" screamed the panic-stricken woman.

"Come back here!" yelled the officer.

"Oink!" said Oinky, watching them go and then looking around him. They were in a small street which was lined with shops of all kinds and the pavements were lined with people. One or two started to point at this pink pig as he sat in the front seat of a Mercedes Convertible, looking at them over the steering wheel. On the seat next to him, a mobile phone started to ring and he nudged it with his nose.

"Hello?" said a voice.

"Oink," said Oinky as he sniffed and then picked it up in his teeth. As the pig climbed out of the car and wandered out on to the street, people started to run and shout in general panic.

"Hello? Carol, is that you?" said the phone in Oinky's mouth.

Now at eight am in the morning in a suburban street in a city, the sight of a talking pig might look somewhat peculiar. Let's face it, the sight of a talking pig at any time of the day would be somewhat peculiar.

"What time will you arrive, have you brought the whip?" said Oinky to a tall thin man wearing a turban. The man ran for cover behind the bus shelter as Oinky looked up at him with his piggy eyes.

"Our baby will soon be starting," he said to young plump woman, "you must get here quickly!" The woman screamed. In fact there was quite a lot of screaming in the district of Pemberton on that sunny summer morning. It wasn't long before the screaming of a police siren added to the din as well, its flashing blue lights reflecting from the shop windows and turning Oinky from pink to blue and back again, every other second. The pig looked up at the shop window that was offering roast sandwiches. He couldn't read the sign obviously, but a roast pork sandwich is pretty recognisable in any language, possibly due to its smell. Oinky definitely didn't like this smell, as he poked his head in through the door to see a half roasted pig revolving on a spit. The man in white overalls looked down at Oinky holding a long pointy knife. Oinky knew about knives and decided this was not a good place to be.

"Don't move, you are surrounded!" shouted a voice through a megaphone.

"Where the blazes are you?" said Oinky.

"We are over here!" called out the policeman, replying to the talking pig.

"Who is over where?" replied the pig.

"Don't try to be smart?" said the amplified voice.

"What?" said Oinky.

"You heard me, don't try to do anything smart! You are surrounded!" Oinky looked up at the two men in blue uniforms who were closing in on him. With that and the butcher in the shop, his mind agreed that he was indeed surrounded. His mind also deduced that perhaps it was time he was somewhere else.

"Alright, must dash, we are under starters orders!" called out the mobile phone, just as Oinky started to run. As he galloped down the street he dropped the mobile phone from his mouth which shattered on the pavement. There were still quite a lot of people on the street and these quite a lot of people were still doing quite a lot of shouting. Oinky ignored them, as he squeezed between legs and prams in his efforts to escape being captured. He was scared, but then he was often scared. A large red lorry with windows in it loomed alongside the curb next to him. It had a side door and a low platform near to the ground, so Oinky jumped on and then dived in behind a row of seats.

"Stop or I will shoot," shouted the policeman. This made people in the street panic even more. Some were even lying on the ground when the two officers arrived at the bus stop out of breath. Their police training had not prepared them to run after wild animals and they were no match for a young pig which was running for its life. They looked around and then at the people standing there. It seems that nobody had noticed where the pig had gone. It had sort of vanished.

"Maybe it had gone down that alley?" suggested one bystander, pointing to a dark alleyway between some shops. "It had possibly crossed the road and headed down Neville Street?" offered another. The two police officers looked at each other, one scratching his head, and then one signalled for the other man to check out the alleyway.

"It has to be here somewhere?" shouted the officer, through his microphone to a poor confused old lady. She hit him with her handbag.

"No need to shout!" she told him.

Oinky lay under the seat, shivering silently for some time. Nobody had seen him get on the bus as it was so crowded. He peered out to see rows of legs rocking from side to side as the vehicle lurched around the corners. When it came to an abrupt halt, a little bell sounded and a voice shouted out from the front.

"This stop, Barnton. This bus will be calling at Ribitch, Tasely, Lower-Highmarsh, Higher-Lowmarsh and Hanley William, before reaching its final destination at Weston-on-the-mere!"

Some people got off and some more people got on, there was a bit of shuffling, some exchange of seats, then the bell sounded again and the bus lurched forward once more. Nobody noticed a small pig under seats number 32 and 33, although one or two people had complained about a rather unusual smell.

9

Ricky Warner had been a bin-man for most of his life. He hadn't set out on a career in dustbins, it just happened that way. His real ambition was to be in the army like his brother, but they wouldn't let him in because of his eyesight. But that hadn't stopped Ricky from being a soldier, except for him it was just on weekends with his mates in the forest, when they would blacken their faces and go hunting. There wasn't a lot to hunt in the Forest of Dean, but the men enjoyed it; the odd pheasant here, a pigeon or perhaps a rabbit there. Last year one of them had shot a wild boar; well, it wasn't so much as a wild boar, more of a roaming pig that may possibly have belonged to the farm nearby. He and his mates had taken it down to that shop in Pemberton in the back of Ricky's old van and got good money for it.

As the big dustbin wagon pulled to a stop near the end of the promenade, Ricky jumped down and grabbed at the black refuse sacks, slinging them up into the back of the lorry with practised ease. He was a fit man for his years and the job gave him a good chance to exercise. As he threw the next sack, the bottom fell out of it and rubbish spilled out all over the road. Ricky cursed at this and grabbed his broom from the lorry, sweeping it up.

"Damn vermin, tearing the bags open!" he said, "probably foxes or badgers!" When he returned to collect the last of the sacks he saw something moving in the shadows. A lesser man that Ricky may have jumped back, or even run away, as the wild animal amongst the sacks stirred from its sleep and made a wild animal-like sound.

"Oink!" said Oinky, opening his eyes. As his eyes focused he saw a man in khaki trousers with budging tattooed arms, about two feet away. The man had a knife. Oinky often dreamt about men with knives so it took him a few seconds longer than normal to start squealing, but squeal he did, very loudly. The man dived and caught him around the hind leg. Oinky's mind raced. The last time someone had tried to cut him he had bitten them on the hand and this tactic had worked. He tried it again on this man, his sharp teeth sinking into the man's flesh. Only this time, the man just grinned at him with wild eyes and then used his other hand to grab Oinky around the back of the neck.

"Hah, we got ourselves a live one!" shouted Ricky, as he dragged the squealing pig from the comfort of its bed amongst the rubbish sacks. "Live and kicking!" Oinky was indeed alive and kicking; kicking with all his might. As the man looked closely at him, another man appeared alongside him.

"Wut you got ther?" said the other man, wearing a baseball cap and a vacant expression.

"What's it look like?" said Ricky.

"Uhh, luks like a piggy?"

"Not just any piggy, you dumbwit, this is a real live wild boar!"

Now I am not sure if you have ever encountered a real live wild boar, I suspect not. The thing about real live wild boar is that they generally don't live in towns, they are quite large and very fierce. The thing about the so-called wild boar that Ricky was holding *was* in a city and it wasn't very large, quite the opposite in fact. But it was fierce, or at least it was trying vey hard to be. The squealing got louder as Oinky writhed and thrashed about under the man's tough grip.

"Wut cha going ta do with it?" asked the other man, slowly. Ricky was thinking the same question. He didn't think this small animal would be of any interest to the butcher, he wasn't sure it was any interest to anyone. But he had caught it, Ricky the soldier, Ricky the hunter. This was his prey and he needed to make sure everyone saw that.

"Can you finish the bin collection for the last two streets by yourself, Dan?" He looked at the less intelligent man who nodded from behind his thick glasses. "Thanks pal." Ricky reached into his pocket and pulled out his mobile phone as Oinky squealed and squealed. "Hey, Babe?" he called out above the noise when a woman answered. "What? The noise? Oh, it's my new pet. No, it's not a dog. I know you don't want us to have a dog, so I got somefing else instead. Can you bring the van down to the corner of Ebbings road. It's alright, I will tell you all about it." Oinky squealed again. "And make it quick, Babes, I am getting deafened!"

Ricky had covered the noisy small pig in his jacket while he waited for his girlfriend to arrive. Oinky didn't like being covered up and squealed even more, his muffled noise echoing around the concrete precinct, while Ricky looked around shiftily, checking his wrist-watch. It was a good ten minutes before the van arrived and Oinky was bundled into the back.

As the white rusting van trundled down Weston promenade, anyone watching it from behind would have seen the face of a small pig looking out through one of the rear windows. Oinky's nose twitched as he viewed the big blue ocean and its long golden sandy beach. He had had an interesting evening mooching about the town before settling in for the night amongst the rubbish sacks. He had certainly been well fed, there were more scraps than he could have dreamt of. And he *had* dreamed of food; food and men with knives. As Oinky's dreams went, this had been quite a good one compared to some he had, and in his dream he was being fed on bread and tomatoes. If only he could have woken up a bit sooner, he wouldn't have been in this situation now. Here he was, imprisoned in the back of a van by a very strong and rough man. He had no idea where he was headed but suspected it wouldn't be good, as the van turned steeply up a hill so the sea was now far below them. The woman in the front of the van kept peering round at him and smiling.

"E's gorgeous, Ricky. So cute!" she had told the man when she first arrived. Oinky had been squealing then but she had stroked his face and his back, and he had quietened down a bit. The woman had kind eyes and milky blonde hair. She also had a nice smile and Oinky quite liked it when people smiled at him. People who smiled generally didn't want to kill, did they? He wasn't so sure about the man but, he deduced in his little brain, if the man had wanted to kill him he may have done so already, with his big knife. The woman threw him another piece of stale bread and Oinky gobbled it up. "So cute," she said again.

"Well, we will have to fatten him up a bit before we can sell this one," said her partner, glancing at the pig in his mirror.

The road they were travelling on turned more into a bumpy track and the sides of the van rattled as the speeding vehicle raced along it, leaving a cloud of dust behind. Oinky's hooves slipped sideways on the vans wooden floor, while he looked out of the back window at the great mountains of sand and grass as they passed. Eventually they came to a gate and rumbled over a cattle grid before coming to a halt beside a grey caravan. Ricky folded down the front seat of the van and climbed into the back, his jacket at the ready. Oinky tried to dash past him and escape through the front door but, once again, the man was too quick and smothered him with the coat. He started squealing again, as he was dragged from the van and carried under Ricky's arm. A dog was barking fiercely and Ricky shouted at it to be quiet but it took no notice. Then the man opened the door to a small shed, pulled off the jacket and threw Oinky inside onto a dirt floor. The door slammed shut behind him as he lay there shivering with fear, and adjusting his eyes to the dim light. There were no lights or windows, just a gap under the door and a tiny hole in the roof that allowed enough daylight to seep in. Outside, the dog pushed its nose close to the bottom of the door and growled viciously before barking again. It didn't sound friendly, in fact Oinky had never heard an animal so angry before; he was terrified. In the interests of his own safety, he kept well away from the door and hid behind some large barrels, squeezing himself between two plastic sacks and staying still. It was a while before the dog gave up interest and quietened down. Oinky peered out from between the sacks until he could no longer see the shadow of the dog's nose at the door and his nose twitched as he sniffed the damp air in the shed. There was a very nice smell coming from the barrels, a sort of musty sweet smell. As he squeezed his little body out from between the sacks one of them toppled over and a pile of apples spilled out on to the dirt floor of the shed. Oinky sniffed one of them and pushed it along the ground with his nose before grabbing it in his mouth. He had never eaten apples before but this one was quite tasty and it made a loud crunching sound as he chewed it up, juice dripping down his chin.

He was half way through the first bag by the time the door opened again and the woman's face appeared in the light. She put a bucket of water down on the floor, her eyes squinting when she looked over to the back of the shed at the small pig. He looked up at her for a few seconds as she smiled at him, a red and green apple between his jaws.

"Hey, you are not supposed to be eating those!" she yelled out, the smile disappearing from her face. Oinky dropped the apple from his mouth when he heard the shouting; he didn't like being shouted at so he scurried back in behind the large barrels once more and hid until the woman closed the door. The dog started barking again as the woman shouted outside. "Ricky, you had better come here, now!"

Oinky's stomach started to feel full and he decided not to eat any more apples. He was just lying down amongst some sacks when the door opened again and this time Ricky came running in.

"You damn pig, those were my best cider apples," he snarled, "they make the finest scrumpy in the whole South West, those apples do!" Ricky started picking up the remaining apples and stuffing them back in the bag as Oinky hid behind the barrel. Then he squealed loudly when Ricky grabbed him and even tried to bite the man as he picked him up by the ear. "Come on, you can't stay in here!" The man squeezed his stomach and Oinky let out a rather unsavoury smell. These apples were starting to feel heavy in his belly as they swished and swilled about like socks in a washing machine. Maybe he had eaten a few too many? Oinky looked down at the large black dog when Ricky carried him out into the light. The dog had a long pointed brown nose and very sharp teeth which snapped up at his heels.

"Ringo, get down will you!" shouted the man to the dog. Oinky noticed it had a thick leather collar around its neck attached to a chain. Once they went around behind the caravan the dog reached the end of its chain and started to bark again.

Soon, the dog wasn't the only one to be wearing a collar. Oinky tried his best to stop the man attaching it around his neck but it was no use. Once it was secured, Ricky dropped him down on to the grass and as soon as he hit the ground Oinky started to run. He gathered speed as he raced through the sand and grass, not daring to look round. He was a good twenty metres away when the chain reached its full length and the collar pulled tight around his neck. Oinky pulled and pulled but it was no use, he could go no further. He lay on the ground and squealed.

10

Violent gusts of wind whipped the sand around the dunes like a snow storm. The sun had been beating down for days but now this wind brought with it the threat of rain. A blizzard of dust blew from the top of the small hill above Oinky's head as he buried himself in the cool sand below. The prickly grains had got into his eyes and embedded in his hair and skin, as Oinky lay out there tied to his chain.

Shortly after, a few spots of rain dropped from the sky as he opened his eyes a fraction. The rain soon got heavier and Oinky shifted his body in the bed of sand he had been sleeping in.

"Oink," he said excitedly, and jumped to his feet. His chain rattled beside him when he stepped out from under the grassy sand dune and felt the lovely rain washing into his scalp. It was time for his morning run but it could wait for a while, as Oinky had his first shower in over two weeks. He looked across to see the wisps of smoke from the chimney on the caravan a few hundred metres away, and a light was on inside, but he didn't think his breakfast would arrive for a while yet. Darkening skies overhead suggested that this was not just a light shower but a really heavy storm. A couple of weeks earlier there had been a few days of rain and Oinky had snuffled in the ground by a low place nearer to the caravan, churning it into mud. It had dried out since but now the rain would wet it again and that was how Oinky liked it. The little pig's ears flapped up and down as he raced through the downpour and threw himself into the cool muddy puddles, rolling around on his back and oinking happily while the sticky mud clung to his skin. Within a short stretch of time he had turned from sandy-gold to pinky-white and now to a lovely shade of brown.

It had taken Oinky a few days to get used to being tied up on a chain and at first he had hated it. Ricky and the woman had placed a bucket of water in the field which was within his reach and had brought him food three times per day. The food was mainly scraps and leftovers but some of it was quite tasty. On the other side of the caravan was the fearsome dog, chained up, and it had barked every time Oinky had gone near, making every meal time a bit of a trial. That is why he spent most of his time over by the sand dune where he had dug himself a shelter out of the soft sand. He liked it in there as it was cool protection from the hot sun but also it muffled the noise from the rabid dog.

After his very first breakfast, the dog had scared him, as it had poked its nose out from under the caravan and barked its angry threats right out in front of him. Oinky had run away as fast as he could but, as the chain stopped him from going too far, his running had taken him around in a large circle and within a minute he was back where he started. As the days went on, this had become a bit of a habit and Oinky would take his morning run around the circuit before and after breakfast. He liked the exercise and it kept him fit. It also stopped him gaining too much extra weight.

Ricky scratched his head when he arrived with the bucket of feed and saw the pig wallowing in the muddy hollow. It had been nearly three weeks and the pig didn't seem to be gaining weight at all, despite the amount of food he had been given. When Oinky saw him he splashed out of the mud and ran over to the food, gobbling it down with great speed as the rain fell in torrents from the sky. Ricky turned and rushed back into the caravan. He didn't think he wanted to go to work today, he would phone in sick. Now he stood in his kitchen watching the pig gobble its food and wondering what he should do with the creature. His girlfriend, Holly, had loved the pig at first, stroking it and saying how cute it was. But she had lost interest now the novelty of having a pig in the field had worn off. She had lost interest in the animal and in him as well. In fact he hadn't seen her for a few days and suspected she must have another boyfriend somewhere. Just as he was about to sit down to his cup of tea, he saw the pig finish its food and then take off at great speed. Rubbing his eyes and hardly believing what he was seeing, he watched Oinky set off around the circuit, his chain pulling tight the whole way. Ricky had never seen an animal move so fast, as the surefooted pig passed the window for the third time. He scratched his head again. So that's why the animal hadn't put on any weight? He was running it all off again with this exercise. And the animal seemed to be enjoying itself too, oinking away happily. Ricky was most concerned. He would have to put a stop to this. He couldn't put the pig in the shed as it had already eaten some of his best apples. Anyway the shed was now full of cider, since he had bottled it out of the barrels. There was good money to be made in cider; he should be able to sell this whole batch at the fair later this week. No, there was no way the pig was going in there. When the rain stopped he would have to get rid of the pig once and for all. Ricky couldn't carry on feeding it if the thing wouldn't get fat. He made up his mind to do it that evening as he drained his tea and went back to bed.

Later that afternoon, Ricky loaded 6 bottles of his new cider into his van and drove down to the Kings Head. He was to meet up with his hunting buddies who were going to taste his cider to see if it was up to scratch. If it was anything like as strong as last year they would all be half-drunk by 6 o'clock and he hoped that would be a good advert for his product. He may even persuade the landlord to buy some from him and sell it over the bar. Later, he would come back up here and finish the pig off with his rifle. Perhaps his mates would come along as well and they could try and shoot it on the move; that would be a laugh!

At five-thirty, the three men were sitting on the red leather bench by the window, draining their second glass of cider. One of them wore a leather hat and had a straggly beard. He was entertaining the others, and most of the rest of the clients in the pub, by singing a folk song and accompanying himself on a guitar. Ricky and his other friend joined in at the chorus, banging their hands on the table as it finished. An older man in a trilby hat watched them from a bar stool.

"Decent cider then, is it lads?" he said in an Irish brogue.

"The best scrumpy in the whole South West," replied Ricky, slurring his words slightly. "You wanna buy some?"

"Not if it makes me sing as badly as your three," chuckled the Irishman, picking up his pint of Guinness. The three lads looked up at the man sitting at the bar. Ricky didn't like being insulted like that and he reckoned they might have to teach this stranger a lesson.

"Who are you then? Can you sing any better?" said the slightly drunken Ricky, standing up and wobbling a bit. "Coz if you can't, you had better shut your mouth!"

"Now lads, we don't want any trouble," said the landlord of the pub, spotting that there may be a fight. The Irishman took off his trilby hat and stepped off the bar stool, smiling. Ricky looked up at him, all three of them looked up at this stranger; he was huge, possibly six-feet-six or more. The man flexed his tattooed knuckles and the landlord got ready to phone for the police. Then the Irishman put his hand inside his coat, reaching for something as the landlord started dialling nine-nine-nine, assuming this stranger was reaching for a weapon.

"No, we don't want no trouble, to be sure," he boomed and produced a half sized violin from inside his jacket. A big grin spread across the man's face as he held the instrument up to his chin. With his other hand he pulled a string bow from down his trouser leg and started playing. The tune was a slow melody and the man's big fingers danced on the neck of the violin as the beautiful notes rang out around the bar. Everyone fell silent and Ricky sat back down on his chair. The landlord stopped dialling and replaced the receiver as he watched this stranger start to sing:

Over in Killarney
Many years ago,

Me Mither sang a song to me
In tones so sweet and low.
Just a simple little ditty,
In her good auld Irish way,
And I'd give the world if she could sing
That song to me this day.

"Come on lads, help me out wit the chorus now?" he called to Ricky and his friends.

Too-ra-loo-ra-loo-ral, Too-ra-loo-ra-li,
Too-ra-loo-ra-loo-ra, hush now, don't you cry!
Too-ra-loo-ra-loo-ral, Too-ra-loo-ra-li,
Too-ra-loo-ra-loo-ral, that's an Irish lullaby

By the time the stranger had finished this song many of the men and women in the pub had tears in their eyes because the song had been so sad. There was a deadly silence followed by raucous applause as the big man put away his tiny instrument and sat back down on the bar stool. Ricky and his friends looked at each other and then got up to leave. They had a job to do that evening and it would be fun. No time to sit around and listen to this stranger warbling on.

"That's an Irish lullaby," he said when the landlord asked the man what the song was called, "and mine's a pint o Guinness!"

The landlord poured him the pint. "What brings you to these parts then?" he enquired, casually.

"Oi am just here for the fair this week. Pat McGowan is the name, Oi am in the entertainment business." He held out his hand for the man to shake.

"You certainly can sing a good note."

"What? That? No, Oi am not a singer, that is just a song my old Dad taught me. No, Oi run a pig racing business!"

"Pig racing?" said the landlord loudly.

"To be sure, tis a big sport where Oi come from," said the Pat. Ricky was halfway out of the door when he heard this and he turned on his heel. Here was a man he suddenly needed to talk to.

* * * * *

Ricky Warner winced with pain when Pat McGowan nearly crushed his hand, as they shook on the deal. He couldn't believe his luck when he had met this stranger in the pub earlier and had persuaded him to come back with him to the caravan. Pat had driven them there in his new Range-rover. The nearer they got to the caravan, the more the cider had given Ricky confidence, especially as Pat drove such a flash car.

Oinky had been lying in the hollow when they arrived, and was covered in mud from head to toe. Ricky had shouted at him so he had gone and hidden under the shelter of the sand dune. All the while the dog had been barking and it took quite a lot of persuasion to get him to come out, but eventually one thing had tempted him. That thing had been a very large man offering him his all-time favourite food. Cream crackers. Oinky oinked happily as he munched them out of the man's hand one at a time, all the time watching Ricky and keeping an eye out for the dog.

"He's only a baby," said the Irishman, looking at the scrawny pig. "He wouldn't be any use to me, Oi couldn't put him on the track, he would get laughed at."

Oinky didn't like the idea of being laughed at and he ran away as fast as he possibly could. In fact he was round the circuit so quickly that the two men had to jump out of the way as he came speeding by a second time, mud flying up behind him.

"He is the fastest pig in the South West," said Ricky, trying to persuade the man, "and he is yours for a hundred pounds."

"A hundred pounds?" said the Irishman, "and there was me thinking we would be doing some business together. Oh well, Oi'll be seein ya!" The big man strode off towards his vehicle without looking back, a cunning smile on his face. Ricky realised that maybe he had asked for a bit too much money for the pig.

"OK, make it seventy five!" he called, hopefully, starting to chase after Pat, who had kept on walking. "Sixty five, my best price. You are getting a bargain at that. The fastest pig in the South West," pleaded Ricky.

Pat McGowan listened to the little man from the South West trying his best to make a deal. Pat was good at making deals. All his life he had made deals. All his life he had made money. He opened the door to climb in to the Range-rover as Ricky caught up with him. His eyes narrowed as he looked down at the younger man.

"The pig is too small, but Oi will take him off your hands for twenty-five pounds," he said, holding out his big tattooed hand. "That, or nothing!"

Ricky's hand was still hurting as the two of them reeled in the pig on its chain like pulling a fish from the sea. Pat stroked Oinky as he looked up at him, before picking him up with one hand around the back of his neck and unclipping the chain. When they reached the car, he opened the boot and pulled out a hessian sack, which he effortlessly stuffed Oinky into before placing him in the boot. Oinky squealed at first but then, as the boot lid closed down, he went quiet. The dog was still barking outside as the big car rode away down the muddy track. That was one place Oinky had been glad to leave.

Pat McGowan sang to himself as he guided the car down the lane and on to the main road. "What aboutcha?" he called to the pig in the back. "Do you loik me singin, or what?"

"Oink," said Oinky as he headed towards his new career as a racing pig.

11

"Roll up! Roll up!" shouted a loud voice. "Next show starts at eleven thirty!" Pat looked at the young woman doing the shouting. He had met Daisy in a bar in Dublin or, to be precise, he had met her mother in a bar in Dublin and she had begged him to give Daisy a job.

Pat McGowan had been born in a tiny village just outside Cork in Southern Ireland. He had always worked hard, right from when he was a lad working on farms. At eighteen years old he had saved enough money to take a passage to America and had landed in New York without money or a job. This hadn't worried Pat and he soon found work as a builder, working high up on scaffolding platforms as they built new skyscrapers. After a couple of years he became foreman and a couple of years after that, he started his own building company. Business was good for a while until Pat got fed up with living in the city and bought a small farm near a town called Glenwood in the state of Iowa. It didn't take Pat long to fit into local life and he soon stocked his farm with animals. At first it was just cattle and a few sheep, but then he branched into breeding pigs. He first got the idea about pig racing when watching the little piglets run around the field chasing each other. He tried a few experiments and set up a track at his home, inviting his neighbours round to have a look. Soon the word got around about this new and interesting sport and Pat started to hold monthly races. He realised that everyone was prepared to bet on the pigs and it wasn't long before he was charging folks an entrance fee. Within a year, Pat McGowan's PIG-

FAST company was up and running, using a lorry and some mobile railings. As Pat was starting to find life on a farm in Iowa quite lonely, he took it on the road.

"Roll up, Roll up, see the amazing racing pigs," shouted Daisy, waving her Pig-fast flag high in the air. "Betting shop opens in ten minutes." Daisy had always been a bit of a loner, growing up in Dublin. She had been in and out of trouble for much of her life, just small things; fights at school, stealing a few sweets, scrumping apples, that sort of thing. At the age of twelve she had decided she didn't want to go to school any more; they never really taught her anything useful. She was better at maths than anyone in her class, better than the teacher even. Daisy had never met her father but she reckoned her sharp brain must have come from his side of the family. For much of her younger life, Daisy had hung about the house while her mother was either out or asleep. Her mother called herself Rene Raffertey these days, she was a singer, she had always been a singer. The woman had changed her name so many times that Daisy had to think hard to remember what her real name actually was, Paula, that was it, Paula O'Leary. That was Daisy's real name, Daisy O'Leary. But Daisy hadn't liked her real name either and now she was on the road, she thought it was best to change it. Daisy May, that is what she called herself now. Daisy couldn't wait to leave Dublin; she couldn't wait to leave Ireland. Her mother had met this strange man in a bar, an Irish American, who could play the fiddle and charm the ladies. Paula had fallen for him instantly and the two of them had spent a few weeks together. Daisy quite liked Pat McGowan, he was kind and strong and she was pretty sure she could trust him. So, with her mothers blessing, at fourteen years old, she had set off on the road with this man and his strange pig racing business. Pat paid her quite well and she got a small share of the profits. She had her own room inside the big trailer that they travelled in, although sometimes they got to stay in nice hotels instead. The two of them had been on the road for four months now, touring the local agricultural shows and fairs, never staying anywhere more than a week. That was the way she liked it, that way nobody could track her down or pin her down to one place. She had cut her dark curly hair very short and now wore it spiked up with gel. Most of the punters thought she was a boy in her baggy sweatshirt and jeans, but she didn't care. Daisy was more than a match for any boy; in fact she was more than a match for most people.

"Roll up, Roll up, place your bets now, Ladies and Gents," she called out. "You Sir, would you like to see the race schedule, maybe study a bit of form?" The man smiled at her and nodded his head. "That will be a pound, Sir," she said, as she handed him a small folded piece of cardboard with details of all the race runners on it. "We got a new one running today. A complete outsider he is, never run before. An outside bet, but really good odds. Sixteen to one!"

The sixteen to one outsider quivered in his little pen inside the huge trailer. There were eight other pigs in the trailer with him, each one having its own individual pen. He had been put in the trailer that morning, but for the past two days Oinky had been outside with the others in a small enclosure and allowed to run around. In fact he had to run around as the other pigs often chased him. They were all bigger than Oinky; maybe no older, but certainly bigger. They had tried to steal his food but Oinky wouldn't allow that and gobbled it up as fast as he could. At night, he had slept on his own at one end of the railed off piece of grass while all the others huddled together for warmth. During the next day they had teased Oinky and laughed at him because he was so small. "Why would a runt like you be in our racing stables?" they had said. Oinky was thinking the same thing. It wasn't until they got out on to the track that they understood why.

"Roll up! Roll up! Place your bets. You, young man, would you like to see the little piggies?" Daisy smiled at a young boy about 6 years old, "you come and stand at the front here so you can get a better view." The boy shuffled close to the railings. "That'll be two pounds, please," she said to the boy's father, holding out her hand.

The pig racing track was quite a simple affair. It was a circle of metal railings about 25 metres in diameter and around the outside were raised platforms from where folks could watch the races. Pat McGowan was a clever businessman and not only charged people to watch, but charged them for the folded piece of cardboard with names of the runners on it, as well as charging extra for the front stands. But Pat McGowan made most of his money from all the betting that took place. With five pigs in each race, he usually had a pretty good idea of which one was going to win and rigged the odds accordingly. And on top of that, all the local fairs and agricultural shows paid him a fee to turn up with his special attraction! Yes Pig-Fast was a very profitable little operation and today, with his new addition, it may even get better.

Up until now his other eight pigs had all been identical; Pat was very particular about that. The only way that the watching audience could tell them apart was by the number strapped to their back. So, although the race schedule card detailed the animals by name and mentioned how many races they had won in the past, it was never necessarily the same pigs. For example, in the race schedule it said that Artimis, number 6 had won seven times in the last two weeks, so it was pretty obvious that he was an athletic animal with a winning streak. He was the one that most people would bet their money on, even though his odds were only two-to-one. Two-to-one meant that if a punter bet one pound on that pig and it won the race, they would get two pounds in return. However, Dollar, Number 4, had not won a race for weeks, so his odds were ten-to-one. Although this meant that a one pound bet could win you ten pounds if Dollar romped home in first place, it was pretty unlikely that he would, so very few people put a bet on him. Gambling is a funny business.

Five of the pigs were shuffled into five little crates at the start of the track, as the crowd queued up, paying their money to the young girl. Pat sat in his little booth near to the railings and accepted the bets, handing out a ticket to each one as he took their money.

It wasn't difficult to teach a pig how to race; Pat had found a simple technique which involved food. Pigs are, by nature, a greedy animal, and greedy animals will run after food. To begin with Pat had trained them by dragging a cabbage around the track at high speed, so the pigs would chase it and, when they reached the end of the race, there would always be a bowl of corn and cabbage waiting for them to eat. Very soon it was not necessary to drag the cabbage around at all, as the pigs would race round the track in a hurry just to reach the bowl of food. On the morning of the race, the pigs were not allowed any breakfast and basic hunger would drive them on as soon as the trap was opened and they were released.

"Ladies and Gentlemen, welcome to the Pig-fast extravaganza!" shouted Daisy to the hundred of people watching from the stands. She was now speaking into a microphone so that her voice could be heard echoing around the show field. "Let me introduce to you, the runners in the first race. In lane one, we have DOLLAR!" the crowd clapped for Dollar although they could see that she wasn't a particularly good runner, judging by her past history. "In lane two, we have Razmus!" The crowd clapped again, Razmus was a young pig who may soon show a bit of promise, so it said on their piece of cardboard. "In lane three, we have Artimis the wonder pig!" The crowd roared and cheered when they heard his name. This was the pig most of them had bet their money on, he was hot favourite. The other two lanes had Sandman and Horatio.

Inside the trailer, Oinky could hear all the shouting and introductions being made. He wasn't really sure what was going on, it was all very new to him. A couple of times he had been let out on the track and had not needed much encouragement to run around it. Oinky liked running, especially if it meant there was food at the other end. Then he heard a gun shot and the nice girl shout out: "And they're off!" Oinky didn't like the sound of the gun shot and then lots of people shouting, so he hid his head under the straw in his little pen, as the other three pigs in the trailer jumped up and down with excitement.

The race didn't take very long as the crowed whistled and cheered. "And the winner is….. Artimis. Give him a big cheer!" The crowd cheered alright, most of them had won a pound. This pig racing was fun *and* they could make some money! This wasn't gambling, this was betting on a dead certainty, or so they thought. Soon afterwards a queue formed outside Pat's little booth and he paid out two pounds to each of the winning bets, smiling politely as he did so.

12

Oinky hadn't needed to have a number strapped to his back, it was fairly obvious which one he was; he was the one with the missing tail. He peered out through the door of the trailer as Daisy tried to tempt him out with some cream crackers. "Come on little one, I know it's your first time but don't be shy."

"Oink," he said, quietly, when he appeared on the ramp and looked around nervously at all the people. The crowd burst out laughing and he darted back in again and hid under the straw.

"Ladies and Gentlemen, please try and be quiet, this is his first race and I think he is a little nervous." Daisy tried again to tempt Oinky with some cream crackers and he followed the trail of broken ones out into the doorway. This time the crowd were silent as he stepped out into the light, oinking quietly to himself. Daisy sprinkled a trail of biscuits down the ramp and he followed them all the way into the race-trap in lane five. The door snapped shut behind him and he squealed in fright when he realised that it actually was actually a trap. Around him, the crowd roared with laughter again. This little pig was so funny with its twitching nose and stunted body. Four other larger pigs were lined up in the race-traps either side of him and they were sniggering too. They had done this a hundred times before and all of them enjoyed the noise of the roaring crowd and the bucket of food at the other end of the track. Daisy introduced the other pigs. Dollar was running again, this time in lane one, then Kato, Bungle and Maximus, the young pig with a future. "And now in lane five we have our new member. He doesn't have a name yet, so as a special treat for you lovely audience here in Weston, we will hold a competition for you to give him a name. Please fill in the box on the back of your race schedule and hand it in at the booth along with the one pound entry fee." Pat was so clever that he would easily earn the cost of buying Oinky by taking money from these people, before the pig had even run a race.

"Ladies and Gentlemen, as our new contestant is a novice, we are offering odds of sixteen-to-one for him to win. That means, if you bet one pound on him, you will get sixteen pounds back!" As Daisy told them this information, it was pretty obvious they were unimpressed. "You could offer five hundred to one if you like," shouted one man in a baseball cap, "that pig ain't never going to win nothing!" The others laughed. Daisy ignored him; she wasn't sure why Pat had entered this little pig in the race either. It was fairly obvious that it didn't stand much chance, but it was quite a sweet little animal and there was something cute about it. It seemed to quite like her too and she almost felt sorry for it.

The girl waited patiently for all the crowd to place their bets in the little booth before raising her small pistol.

"Ladies and Gentlemen, please get ready for the next race. They are under starters orders. Get set...." She fired the pistol in the air and the front of the traps were sprung open. BANG!! Four pigs set off out of the traps like they were possessed by demons. The crowd shouted like they were possessed by demons too. One little pig cowered in his trap, quivering! Oinky didn't like the sound of the gunshot and he certainly didn't like all these shouting people. He was confused and very scared indeed, as he looked out at the other pigs running away around the track. Eventually he poked his head out and looked up at a small boy eating a packet of crisps by the railing. The boy threw one down to him and he gobbled it up. It was then that Oinky remembered about the bowl of food at the other end of the race track and started to run. Nobody really took much notice of him until he was halfway around the track and gaining on the others. Even then it was fairly obvious that he wasn't going to win and they concentrated on the other pigs as they reached the finish line where Pat was waiting with a chequered flag.

"And the winner is...MAXIMUS!!" shouted Daisy after Pat had held up four fingers. "What a close race, Ladies and Gentlemen. Give a big hand for Maximus, a young pig with a future."

Maximus Pork was indeed a young pig with a future. If Oinky was the runt of his litter, then Maximus was the giant of his. He wasn't fat, just big, much bigger than all his siblings. He was also much bigger than Oinky, despite him only being half Oinky's age. Maximus had been chosen personally by Pat McGowan when he was quite tiny, as the big Irishman had spotted some potential in this young pig. Pat had been visiting pig farms throughout Ireland trying to choose his racing stock and he had chosen four from one particular farm, when the tiny Maximus had snuffled around his feet and then sunk his sharp teeth into Pat's boot. Maximus had a habit of sinking his teeth into most things. As Oinky arrived, somewhat late, to the finish line in the second race at Weston Fair, Maximus sunk his teeth into him too, by way of an introduction. Oinky took exception to this and squealed very loudly. Pig's don't have a very large vocabulary and Oinky's was smaller than most. But, if that squeal could be translated into a more comprehensible language such as, say, English, it would have said:

"Arrrggghhh, get off me you big bully, why does everyone keep picking on me?" After which Maximus would have replied:

"You, small creature, are inferior to me in every way. I am Maximus Pork and very soon I will be king of the pig racing world. You, small creature, are not fit to be on the same track as I, Maximus. You could never beat me in this world, or any other." Except that it all sounded like OINK!

Oinky tried very hard to ignore this big bully and ran to his bowl of food, snuffling it down and shivering. He didn't like Maximus and he was very scared of him. In fact, although Maximus was the youngest in the whole team, most of the others were scared of him too. Oinky glanced up to see the pig being awarded with his winner's medal, walking with the style swagger that all winners tend to adopt. Oinky was not a very assertive pig but for once he had an assertive thought and that thought was this. *"One day I will beat that Maximus, if it's the last thing I do."*

The audience was asked to applaud all the pigs, especially the new one who hadn't quite got the hang of it yet. They were told to come back in half an hour's time when the final race would be held, once the racing pigs had chance to rest a while. Young Daisy explained that the last race may be a real thriller between the winners of the first two races, Artimis the wonder pig and Maximus the pig with the future. There was no mention of Oinky, the stunted pig with no tail who had just made himself a promise.

The five pigs were herded back into the trailer, each one into its individual pen. Oinky avoided the glare of Maximus as he passed him, sticking his nose in the air in defiance. There was some grunting and snorting going on between the animals as Pat gave each one of the nine pigs a small bucket of water. Oinky slurped his down as the big Irishman spoke to him.

"You done well there, little pig. Oi reckon there is more to you than meets the eye? The second half of that race, you were running like the wind. And you stood up to Maximus, not many pigs do that!" Daisy was listening at the door of the trailer as she watched the last of the people leave the stands. She had thought the same thing. That small one without a tail seemed to have got the idea halfway through the race and then made up some ground. The girl headed to the front of the trailer and made two cups of tea, taking one back to Pat who was sitting down.

"Are you going to run the new pig in the last race?" she asked, matter-of-factly.

"Well, Oi was considerin it," said Pat, "it will give him some experience. And we need one outsider in the race to keep the punters happy." The girl said nothing, but she was thinking fast. What if the little pig could win a race? At those odds there was some money to be made. She looked out through the trailer door again, straining her eyes looking for someone in particular. He had promised he would be there at 3pm. "Is it alright if I go and have a look around the rest of the fair?" she asked her boss, "I will be back in fifteen minutes." Pat nodded to her, as he closed his eyes for a short knap.

Dave and his younger brother Kev had been to the village dance the night before, the one they held every year before the fair. He had got talking to a young Irish girl with short hair and, the more he had talked to her, the more he had fallen for her. The girl had the most amazing green eyes and such a tender smile, her voice all soft and gentle as tissue. She had said that she worked at the fair and she would be there tomorrow. Dave was not really brave, despite his displays of bravado to the boys at school. Dave was definitely not brave when he was around girls and it had taken all his courage to ask this girl if they could meet up tomorrow. When she had agreed, his heart leapt inside his ribs. The pretty girl had arranged to meet him by the main tent at three o'clock and that was where he was heading now. He fidgeted as he waited, while his younger brother looked bored. Then he saw her, arriving across the field and picking her way through the crowd. Dave realised he had been so nervous the night before that he had forgotten to ask her name. "Kev, isn't it time you went somewhere else?" The younger boy got the message and disappeared just as Daisy arrived.

"Hi," he said, trying to sound cool.

"Darren, isn't it?" she replied, her green eyes flashing in the sunlight. She wasn't very good with boy's names; she had never really found them important.

"Dave," said Dave. "How's it going?" The girl looked nervous, even more nervous than he felt.

"Can we go somewhere?" she said, looking back towards the trailer to see if she was being watched. Dave nodded, his heart pounding once more as they walked away towards the outside of the field. Dave tried to make small talk with Daisy and she sort of listened, nodding her head in the right places as he told her about school and how good he was at football. He had tried to hold her hand but she just brushed her fingers lightly across his palm before drawing it out of his reach. Dave felt his heart race faster and faster as they walked slowly, him talking three to the dozen as she listened. When she smiled at him he thought she was so pretty that he was heart was going to explode. He had never kissed a girl before but something made him desperately want to kiss this one. The more he considered that, the more nervous he became. He was quite taken aback when she suddenly blurted out, "What about gambling, Darren, do you like gambling?"

Dave had never done any gambling before, although he had heard some of the older boys at school making bets on the outcome of football games. It was his turn to listen now, as the girl explained that she worked for a racing stable and that there was a dead cert running this afternoon. She asked him to do her a favour and then slipped two pieces of paper into his hand. "You won't let me down, will you, Darren?" she said, her eyes gleaming like emeralds. Then she reached across and gave him a light kiss, just on the cheek, before turning and walking away. Dave watched her go, speechlessly. He wouldn't wash that cheek ever again. Even if she had gotten his name wrong, he was in love with this girl and he still didn't know what her name was. Dave looked down at the piece of paper in his hand. "Same place, 5pm, don't mess it up now!"

Pat McGowan was quite happy to accept a ten pound bet from the spotty kid with the earring standing in front of the booth. He didn't normally accept bets that big but this bet was on the little pig, the outsider. "Ten pounds on lane five, sixteen to one," he said out loud, as he handed the boy his ticket. Daisy glanced at him briefly but then looked away as the lad smiled up at her. She knew the rules, she wasn't allowed to place bets herself, nor to disclose any inside information to the public.

"Ladies and Gentlemen, place your bets for the last race of the day, the grand final."

Oinky looked out from his little crate at the beginning of the race track. Maximus scowled across at him from the crate next door and then sniffed the air arrogantly. There were three other pigs in the other traps as well, all twitching and snorting as they waited for the final race. After a few minutes Daisy introduced all the runners one at a time. Maximus, Artimis, Dollar, Bungle and the new pig with no name and no tail.

"They are under starters orders, get set....!" Oinky winced as the pistol was fired in the air and the trap door opened in front of him, as the crowd started to shout. But this time he was ready.

"Artimis is in the lead closely followed by Maximus," shouted the girl through her microphone, "they are neck and neck. But hello, what's this, the little pig with no name is gaining on them...." Oinky had learned how to run fast by running away from danger but now he was running fast for a different reason. He came around the inside of the railing like a rocket, oinking for all he was worth as his ears bounced up and down. Maximus glanced sideways and then started to accelerate when he saw this little pig was gaining on him. The bigger pig was in front again but somehow Oinky managed to go faster until he caught him up. It was as though they were in slow motion as Oinky saw the finish line looming up ahead, the two of them running neck and neck. "Go little piggy, go little piggy" shouted out the girl. And he did.

Pat McGowan scratched his head as he watched the little runt of a pig come home in first place. He had only taken one bet on it but it had been quite a big bet. It had certainly taken him by surprise; it had taken everyone by surprise.

"It's a fix!" called out one of the punters.

"The race has been fixed?!!" said another angry loser as he tore up his betting ticket. Pat knew how to fix a race, he had done it a few times before so he could make more money. But this wasn't a fix, it was genuine. Not only genuine but very profitable for Pat, as he would only have one punter to pay and would keep all the rest of the betting money for himself.

Daisy climbed down on to the race track and went across to Oinky who was gobbling down his bowl of food. She held a ribbon in her hand attached to a big shiny medal which she fastened around Oinky's neck. Oinky was quite proud, although the other pigs didn't look too happy about it.

"Give him a big hand. Ladies and Gentlemen, The Pig With No Name!"

One person in the crowd clapped enthusiastically as the others walked away. He was looking at Daisy but again she ignored this kid with the earring, as he called out to her. Pat climbed back into his little booth and the boy went across to collect his winnings. When nobody was watching, Maximus sneaked up behind Oinky and grabbed at the ribbon, tearing it off him and squealing. The squeal probably said something like: *"It's not fair, that should be mine. How dare you beat me.."* Something like that, anyway.

At 5 pm, Dave was waiting by the central tent once again, but this time he had a pocket full of cash. The afternoon had all been a bit of a blur to him and, to start with, he had been so busy watching the girl that he hadn't noticed the little pig with no tail until he saw it arrive at the winning post.

Daisy counted the notes after the boy handed it over, before stuffing it in to her pocket. One hundred and sixty pounds, not a bad days earnings for her ten pound investment. The boy was staring at her and it made her feel a bit uncomfortable. He had gone all dreamy, boys tended to do that round Daisy.

"That little pig," he said eventually, "where did you get him from?"

"I am not sure," she said, "the boss bought him from some local guy. It is a new one, it doesn't even have a name."

"His name?" said Dave Ryan, "I think I know what his name is. It's Oinky Grub. I think he used to belong to my little sister!"

13

By the time George Ryan drove into the field at Weston-on-the-sea with his daughter in the passenger seat, the field was empty except for a few tents.

"It looks like they have gone," he said quietly to Sarah. She could see that already. "Maybe it wasn't him? There are lots of pigs around this area."

"But Dave was sure it was him," she wailed, "he said it was a small pig with no tail. That had to be Oinky!"

"Well, there is not much we can do about it now, I am sorry," replied her father, turning the car around. He had spent the last four weeks looking for the damn creature, as the girl cried constantly. She had said it was all his fault. Everyone had blamed him, even Donna. "We will go out looking again tomorrow," he told her, trying his best to stop Sarah sobbing.

Meanwhile, the big trailer rattled along the M3 motorway as one happy girl and nine reasonably happy pigs slept. Pat McGowan sung quietly to himself. It had been a good weekend. He had made lots of money and taken some more bookings for Pig-Fast show for later in the year. Shortly, he tuned off the motorway, following the signs for the Southampton ferry as the sea loomed up on the horizon.

Daisy woke as the vehicle pulled to a halt at the ferry terminal to see the wide ocean in front of her. She had always loved the ocean; it had always given her a sense of freedom. As a child, while the other children played on the beach, she would sit and look out to sea, always wondering what was over the horizon. Daisy had always felt that life had to better over that horizon. And it had been; so far anyway. Now here she was about to cross the sea again to another land.

This was Oinky's first time at sea and he oinked quietly to himself as the trailer rattled up the metal bridge and into the cargo-hold of the boat. It was dark down there in that hold and he was quite scared so, always looking for an opportunity, the other pigs teased him about this. They said if he was such a champion racer he shouldn't be scared of the dark. But when the big boat started to move, Oinky was even more scared as it rocked the trailer from side to side. Up and down went the boat on the rough seas until Oinky was not only scared but started to feel a bit sick. Except, it wasn't only Oinky that was feeling sick, the other pigs didn't like it either. Maximus squealed and squealed for over an hour in the darkness, and his squeal was really, really loud. It wasn't a pleasant journey across that ocean. Eventually the boat shuddered to a halt with a loud clank as it docked against the platform. Then the bow doors were opened and the light came streaming in at last.

Pat McGowan skilfully manoeuvred the Range-rover and the big trailer out through the bow doors and on to dry land once more. Daisy slid down in the seat as they passed a little glass hut where a man sat in a peaked cap, hoping they wouldn't stop and check her passport. They didn't.

Up ahead, a huge signed spanned the road. It said:

> **WELCOME TO FRANCE,**
> **BIEN-VENUE,**
> **DRIVE ON THE RIGHT**

90

Pat had been used to driving on the right-hand side of the road, that is what they did in America. This was his first time in France too, but he had a booking in central France and the money was too good to refuse. If he could get enough interest he may even start up a whole new racing team based in France. It was yet another opportunity for Pat McGowan, and Pat McGowan was a man of opportunities. He swung the vehicle on to the main auto-route and followed the sign that said: PARIS 200 kilometres.

Daisy couldn't stop smiling as she looked at the little villages as they passed by. France was nothing like she had expected. Its vast flat fields and huge machinery were so different from her home village back in Ireland, where some of the locals still used donkeys to gather the harvest. She was smiling because she had taken a gamble on a little pig and it had paid off, and now she had a pocket full of money. It seemed that the silly boy, Derek, or whatever his name was, had recognised the little pig. He had said it was some kind of fugitive and on-the-run. The little creature didn't seem like a pig on-the-run, it was too pathetic for that. But then, once it got on to that track it had run hadn't it? It had run its little heart out as though it was trying to prove something. Oinky Grub, that's what he had said its name was. That seemed a fitting sort of name for the little creature. She had told Pat that someone in the crowd had recognised the pig, although she hadn't mentioned about her putting a bet on it. Pat had said that nobody would find it where they were going so there was no need to worry.

The vehicle pulled off the motorway and into a service station, nestling the trailer amongst the giant lorries of all different colours. Pat bought nine loaves of bread at the counter, as a few lorry drivers eyed him suspiciously. The bread was strange in this country, not like that in

Britain; the loaves were half a metre long and quite crunchy. One by one, Pat fed each of his racing pigs. Oinky hadn't eaten French bread before but he thought it was quite nice, although not as nice as cream-crackers. It had been a long night for the pigs, since they had run their races the previous day, and now he was extremely hungry. The air was pretty warm in that trailer too, despite it still only being breakfast time, and Oinky was glad of a drink of cool water. Soon the door closed and they were off again, swinging out on to the motorway and gathering speed. The refreshing cool air blew in through the vents on the side of the trailer for another coupe of hours as the pigs all slept again.

The nearer they got to Paris, the more excited Daisy became. She had read about Paris and seen pictures of women in pretty dresses on a street called the Champs Elysee. Pat had bought a map and the girl was looking through it at all the street names. They were going to set up the race at a carnival in the centre of town, in a place called Pigalle. She found it on the map and Pat swung the big vehicle through the busy streets and the rush-hour traffic. It was pronounced *Pig-al*, Pat told her, the Pig-Race in the Pigalle. Daisy squealed with delight when she saw the gigantic Eiffel Tower appear, sticking out above the houses like a giant leafless pine tree. Pat had promised her the afternoon off tomorrow and that was one of the first places she would visit. The Parisian streets were quite busy and narrow and it was nearly lunchtime when they eventually arrived in Pigalle and pulled up outside the hotel. Pigalle district wasn't exactly like she was expecting, and some of the shops looked a bit sleazy with their red curtained windows and bright neon signs. Pat had also bought a French phrasebook and he picked it up from the dashboard of the car as they went inside the hotel reception.

"Bonjour Monsieur, bonjour Mademoiselle," beamed a man in a dark waistcoat.

"Bon-jaw," replied the big Irishman, "Oi think we have a reservation. Mister McGowan and Miss May?"

Daisy was so excited as a boy no older than herself carried her little suitcase up two flights of narrow stairs with her following behind. Her room was a little bit disappointing and not quite as grand as she had hoped.

On one side of a tall narrow window was a small pine table with a golden coloured lamp sitting on it. On the other side, a big old wardrobe lurched slightly to one side, its doors not quite meeting in the middle. She ran to the window, swishing back the dusty curtains and admiring the view, as the boy stood patiently by the door. Daisy pushed her hand into the pocket of her shorts and pulled out a ten pence piece, then, giving the boy one of her best smiles, she pressed it into his hand.

"Thank you," she half sang to him, as he stood there blushing in his silly cylindrical blue hat.

"Merci, Mademoiselle," muttered the bell-boy, looking down at the coin as she closed the door on him. Daisy had only ever stayed in one other hotel in her life, a dingy little place in some dull northern English town which she had forgotten the name of, and even then she had shared it with her boss who had snored all night. But here she was now, in her very own room, in the centre of one of the worlds most wonderful cities, for two whole nights. Daisy did a little dance before flinging herself backwards on to the bed, her arms outstretched wide, and looking up at the high ceiling. She had a whole hour before she needed to go and help Pat feed the pigs and position the trailer. Meanwhile, there was a lot of exploring to do, as she jumped back to her feet and started opening cupboards and drawers. In one draw was a copy of an old magazine called "Paris Match!" which she pulled out and thumbed through its pages, admiring the pretty pictures of classy women posing in tree-lined streets. She looked back out through the window herself and could just about see the top of the large trailer parked outside. A group of scruffy kids had gathered around it. It wasn't her problem, Pat could deal with them.

"C'est les porcs! C'est leg porcs!" called out a boy in the street, as the small crowd gathered around the Pig-Fast trailer. Oinky listened from inside as some of the other pigs slept. He thought he had a vague idea what 'porc' meant and he didn't like the sound of it. Someone banged a stick loudly on the side and all the animals woke up at once. Maximus started squealing, which was a signal for some of the others to start squealing too. Soon the sound of nine pigs squealing echoed around the leafy suburbs of the Pigalle district of Paris. Outside the trailer the young boys laughed and banged some more, until a loud voice boomed at them.

"Get away from there, you urchins, or Oi will tan the lot of yous!" The boys looked up at the giant Irishman shouting at them in a foreign language. The language may have been foreign to them, but the man's intentions were fairly clear. When the lead boy started to run, the others followed him, disappearing from sight in an instance, as Pat unlocked the door to the trailer and peered inside. He spoke soothingly to the pigs to quieten them down and then sat on the steps, looking out at the streets and houses with their lovely wrought iron balconies lining every floor. This certainly was an interesting part of town, with all its brightly coloured shops selling products for adults. They had passed the famous Moulin Rouge a few streets away. Pat had heard of that; just about everyone in the world knew of the

Moulin Rouge and what went on there. Dancing girls and ladies of the night. Pat considered the girl travelling with him, who had sat quietly smiling for most of the way. Daisy was a clever girl but he wasn't sure if he could completely trust the kid, despite her winning smile and bright eyes. Time would tell, but he would have to keep a closer eye on her. Reaching down behind him, the Irishman picked up the small violin and pulled it up to his chin, running the bow over the strings as the simple notes sung out into the quiet street. One of the boys poked his head up from behind the hedge in the park, watching this stranger as he delivered the sweetest of music. Pat liked to play music, it helped him think. He reckoned that the pigs liked it too.

Oinky looked out through the open doorway to the street beyond, oinking quietly as he listened to the soothing music. It had been a long journey and he longed to be outside in the fresh air instead of cooped up his little cage. He wanted to run.

Having explored the inside of her simple bedroom, Daisy was now checking out the rest of the hotel. Further down the corridor was a rickety old lift with a gold painted wire gate that pulled across the front. Climbing inside and closing the gate behind her, she pressed a button and the lift shuddered upwards, squeaking loudly. Excitedly, she watched each of the floors as they passed by, until it clunked to a halt on the top floor. Daisy swung back the gate and rushed to the window to look out. As she had expected, the view from here was magnificent, the Eiffel tower sticking out high above the Parisian streets which were organised in sensible rows. When she opened the big ornate window, Daisy could hear the soothing notes from the violin way down on the street below. A couple of ladies strolled by the trailer, stopping to smile at the Irishman as he played his tune. Nearby, a few old men played a game, throwing heavy round balls into a patch of gravel as they chatted to each other through dense moustaches. Each wore a black beret on their head and the men looked like they had done this every day of their lives, oblivious to the world around them. Yes, Paris was a strange place, where cars drove as fast as fire-engines and yet old men took life so slowly.

14

For those of you who know it, the Pigalle district of Paris looks a lot different at night. For one thing it is swathed in a hue of red light and it also gets a lot, lot busier. Daisy and Pat had worked for a good few hours to get the racing track set up in the centre of the Place de Pigalle, arranging the railings around the huge old fountain. They had even installed a set of bright spotlights so the track could be lit up late into the evening. Loud music was playing and other stalls had set up too, selling candy floss and hot take-away food. Now the tourists and locals were flooding in, many of them looking somewhat confused to see a team of racing pigs confined in a small enclosure behind the big trailer. Oinky looked up pitifully at a smartly dressed couple who peered down at him over the railings. *Oink* he said, in his best French accent. The lady threw him a piece of bread, laughing. *Oink* he said again, *oink oink*, until he received another piece. This was the easiest thing Oinky had ever done.

"Please don't feed the animals," Pat told them. The pigs needed to stay hungry so that they would be racing fit. Daisy connected up the microphone and started calling in the spectators.

"Be-on-von-you!" she shouted, still a bit uncertain about speaking the tiny bit of French she had learned from her phase-book. "Bienvenue! Welcome, to the Pig-Fast extravaganza!" The girl wore a red dress that Pat had bought for her, which was possibly a bit too short for a girl of her age. Daisy didn't like wearing dresses but it was all part of the spectacle. "Voy-ez les cochons de emb-ellage!" She struggled with the words and then tried again in English, "Come and see the racing pigs!"

Pat stepped into the small enclosure and selected 5 pigs for the first race. Oinky was not one of them; he was quite glad of that. While they were away, there would be even more bread for him as the tourists continued to feed this poor half starved little creature with no tail, despite Pat telling them not to. Oinky had never tasted candy-floss before and he quite liked that, chewing the remains from the wooden stick that a child had thrown to him. He ate the stick as well, just in case it was as tasty, but it wasn't.

An assembly of spectators placed their bets on the race, with Daisy calling out encouragement. Soon, a short queue formed outside Pat's little booth as he collected their money and handed out the betting slips. Eventually Pat gave Daisy a nod and she raised her starting pistol and opened the traps, as the pigs bounded out to much applause. As they ran under the bright spotlights, an array of shadows followed them, eerily lining the ground around each one. Maximus Pork was once again the race winner, beating Artimis who came in second again. It was all quite predictable and, amongst all the cheers and applause, Pat made a handsome profit. After they had their feed and Maximus was presented with his winning medal, the five racing pigs were manoeuvred back into the little enclosure, to join Oinky and the other three. There was a short break in proceedings, during which an enterprising man with a large bushy moustache set up a small table nearby, selling red wine in plastic glasses. French people like red wine and just about everybody purchased some. Pat was quite annoyed that he hadn't thought about doing that himself to make an extra profit.

The thing Daisy noticed most about the people of Paris was how smart and well dressed they all were. Young women, old women, they were all so pretty, as they dressed up for every occasion. One or two of the women dressed up a bit too well though, in short skirts, net stockings and bright red lipstick. Daisy had read about them in a magazine. Ladies of the Night, they were known as. Paris was famous for them and, it seemed, this district was most famous of all. Two of them were looking in at the pigs as she watched them, each of them laughing loudly as they held out their cigarettes on long cigarette holders. They were looking at the little pig, the one without a tail. Daisy wondered if she should put another bet on him but guessed that her boss may get suspicious. At least it had a name now.

Oinky gazed up at the two women in red lipstick expectantly, although he couldn't understand what they were saying to him.

'Oink', he replied, courteously, sniffing at a pink high-heeled shoe under the railings. The owner of it squeaked with laughter again and snatched her foot away. Maximus came over to see them too, barging Oinky out of the way as he looked around for bread to eat. Oinky tried to barge him back but the larger pig bit him on the ear and Oinky squealed. Oinky certainly was frightened of this big bullying pig but he also had standards. He plucked up all his courage and bit Maximus back, sinking his sharp teeth into the pig's bottom. This probably wasn't a good idea and the two ladies stepped back when they saw this, suspecting what might happen next. Maximus had just won a race, he was the superior pig and he needed to show it, especially as there was an audience watching. The two pigs started to fight, Oinky biting at everything he could, as the larger pig pushed him to the ground. The sound of squealing echoed out across the streets of Paris, its notes high above the music that was playing. The ladies screamed too, as blood started to fly. People were running. Pat was running. Oinky would have been running if he could. He knew he was beaten but this bigger pig wouldn't let him get to his feet. Oinky didn't much care for the sight of blood, nor the smell of it, especially if it was his own.

Pat McGowan was a strong man, but it took all his strength to pull the bigger pig away from this fight, as it squealed and tried to bite him too. He looked down at the poor smaller one lying in a pool of blood and shivering, shouting for Daisy to help him. A crowd of people had gathered around, talking hurriedly in French and pointing at Oinky. The poor victim opened one eye and looked up at them. He saw the girl bend down over him, putting her hand to a cut on his ear before scooping him up in her arms. A scarlet trail of blood dribbled to the floor as she carried him into the trailer and laid him down on the cold floor. She covered him in a blanket and dabbed at the gash on his ear with a wet cloth as the pig groaned, feebly. Pat poked his head around the door and raised an eyebrow, questioningly.

"He'll be fine" said Daisy, "I just need to stitch up this ear. But I am not sure it is such a good idea to put him in with all the other pigs, he is too small." Pat nodded.

"Keep him in the trailer overnight. He can rest and maybe race tomorrow," said the Irishman, as the girl lifted the first-aid kit down from the shelf. One of the few things Daisy had been reasonably good at, at school, was sewing. Oinky winced as the needle went through his skin, pulling the cut back together and stemming the flow of blood.

100

"There you are, good as new!" smiled Daisy when she had finished. Oinky still kept his eyes closed. Later that evening, he listened to the other pig races going on outside as he lay in the warm trailer, trembling. Maximus, the pig with a future, had won another race, and he was fast becoming top-pig. Oinky considered his standards, keeping a watchful eye on the door. He awaited his next chance. It came quite a few hours later.

Pat was giggling as he opened the door to the trailer. A lady with red lipstick followed him in, a glass in her hand.

"Champagne!" she said in a loud merry voice. "We must 'ave more Champagne, it eez the best drink in the world." Now Pat wasn't much of a man for champagne, Guinness was the only drink he knew, but this lady had won some money on the race and had insisted that they shared a bottle. Inside the trailer was a small living area with a kitchen and some comfy chairs. The painted lipstick lady sat on one of the chairs, but not for very long.

Oink said Oinky. Strangely enough, this took the woman by surprise. She screamed in French. The scream was quite loud and loosely translated to: "Arrrggghhh, there is an animal in here, help get it away from me!" The screaming frightened Oinky, who didn't like screaming. Oinky started squealing. It took Pat a few seconds to realise what was going on. He had forgotten that the girl had put the pig inside the trailer after its fight; but now the pig was now no longer in the trailer. Oinky had seen the open door and he was through it before anyone had chance to consider stopping him. Off he went into the dark Parisian night, squealing for all he was worth.

15

Daisy wandered through the brightly lit streets looking up in amazement. She was seeing things she had never seen before, seeing things she did not even know existed. The Moulin Rouge fascinated her, with its giant red windmill and pictures in the window of dancing girls doing high kicks and showing their underwear. A man stood in the doorway in a red shiny suit, beckoning to her to come in. "Come in and see zee show, it is amazing!" he said to her, his voice purring like a cat. The girl shook her head as she walked on by. Some younger lads leered at her and spoke in French but Daisy just stuck her tongue out at them as she made her way back towards the hotel. It had been a long day and she was tired, but she just needed to check in on the small pig first, to make sure his wound was healing. Daisy had spent much of the evening walking the streets and thinking. She had had enough of pig racing now and the fact that she was in another country and another city; maybe it was time for a change. She had brains, she had some money; there must be opportunities for a bright girl like her in Paris? Daisy didn't really belong with the Irishman and his strange business, Pat could find himself another slave. She looked up from her thoughts when she heard a bit of a commotion up ahead, some shouting coming from near the park, quite a lot of shouting. Daisy just about made out the shape of a pig coming at full speed towards her, its ears bouncing as it ran.

"Arrette, Arrette. Stop ze piggy!" shouted a woman's voice. Oinky went past Daisy so fast that she barely had chance to recognise him, let alone react. She stopped for a second, before turning on her heel and chasing after him.

"Oinky, come back!" she called out, but then considered this. The pig wouldn't come back just because she had called it, it wasn't that clever? Or maybe, it wasn't that stupid? Oinky was running away from something and he looked frightened.

Car brakes screeched on the warm tarmac as a pig ran across the middle of the road chased by half a dozen people. Horns blared and lights flashed as he narrowly missed being squashed by a speeding taxi. Daisy watched Oinky dive out from under its wheels and onto the pavement before disappearing down a narrow alley. They wouldn't catch him, not by running after him shouting anyway. On the corner of the street was a small brightly lit shop which was still open and Daisy slipped inside, unnoticed by Pat McGowan and the couple of other folks who were chasing the pig. She watched them through the window while a neon sign blinked on and off, the men stopping on the corner and looking both ways, peering into the darkness, looking, searching. Daisy had no idea why she did it, but when Pat McGowan walked into that shop to ask the owner if he had seen a small pig running this way, she hid behind a stand of newspapers, watching the shop owner give a shrug and seeing the man leave. Waiting until it was all clear, she then selected a packet of biscuits from a shelf and took them to the counter. The dark haired woman smiled at her as though she had noticed what had happened. A girl hiding from an older man, it was probably commonplace in this part of town? Possibly a girl running from her wicked father, or step-father? Or a girl running from her wicked owner? Who knew what went on in this city? Pat McGowan wasn't a wicked man though, he had

103

been kind to her, but something inside her told her that she wouldn't go back.

Small shops on street corners are much the same the world over, selling a whole host of interesting things, on the off chance someone might suddenly need them. Next to the counter was a card displaying leather dog collars and leads, pretty ones in different colours and sizes. Daisy pointed up to them and the shopkeeper raised an eyebrow.

"It's for my pig!" she said, by way of explanation, the woman then raising both eyebrows. Not being a girl to get bogged down with minor details, she selected a pink check one and a matching lead. It was quite difficult to estimate the size of Oinky's neck and she fumbled with it for a minute, undoing the buckle. Daisy took a guess that his neck was roughly the same size as hers, so she pulled the collar around he own neck, glancing in the mirror as she did so, admiring the pink colour. This time the shopkeeper not only raised her eyebrows, but her eyes nearly popped out of her head. Daisy saw her from the corner of her eye and her own face turned to a pink colour also. "For my pig!" she said again.

After briefly checking through the window that the chasing mob had gone far enough away, Daisy poked her head out of the shop doorway, looking left and right down the street.

"Bon chance!" whispered the shopkeeper, rather uneasily, "good luck!" Giving the woman a polite smile, she headed back into the night once more, clutching her small bag of shopping. Although she didn't know Oinky that well, Daisy had an idea that he was more the sort of animal that would hide rather than keep on running. In a city with thousands of narrow alleyways and cellars, a game of hide and seek would definitely favour the 'hider' rather than the 'seeker'. In fact Daisy didn't really know where to start looking, as she set off down a narrow street next to the convenience store. She questioned the fact that she was looking at all. That pig wasn't really her problem was he? She was her own boss now, free to go, free to roam the country; to explore the world if she chose to. Let's face it, the last thing a young girl with the world at her feet needed was a small stunted pig, with no tail, to tag along. Deeper into the darkness she went, the alleyway getting narrower. Hazy red light glowed from a few of the upstairs windows, lighting up her cheeks and making Daisy feel uncomfortable.

Oinky wasn't feeling too comfortable either, as he nestled in behind a pile of cardboard, burrowing deep until he was out of sight and shivering. Thudding pain in his ear added to his misery, but at least the shouting had stopped. It had been a long day for Oinky and a long night was about to start. He tried to *Oink* himself to sleep, closing his eyes, but it was no good. Every time he did, he saw visions of Maximus biting him and tearing at his ears. Oinky wanted to squeal out, but he knew he must not. His little brain had told him to hide and hide quietly. An hour passed by, while he must have been asleep, before the cardboard beside him started to move, accompanied by the sound of singing. Terrified that it was his captors looking for him, Oinky lay perfectly still and silent, but waiting for his chance to run if he had to.

"Oh la, oh la, c'est mon bon ami.." sang a voice that sounded like it lived on a diet of gravel and whisky. The latter was probably true of Gaston, as he routed about amongst the cardboard, looking for some of the larger pieces to make his bed for the night. Pulling a big box out into the street, the drunken tramp tried to disassemble it, tearing at the corners. With one great pull, the corner came away and Gaston toppled backwards, dropping down into the rest of the pile of rubbish, his head striking on a metal dustbin buried deeper down. The man never heard a pig squealing, despite the fact that it was less than a few inches from his ear, as his world went dark, the bang on his head coupled with a bottle of Bourbon rendering him unconscious. Upstairs, a window flew open and a woman with ginger curly hair and half-naked white breasts peered down to the street to investigate what was happening.

What she saw was a rabid wild animal routing about in the garbage, and a man's body lying in its midst, bleeding. The animal had attacked a human being, killed him by the looks of things. Her screaming added to the din that Oinky was making, echoing down the narrow street until further windows were opened, then even more screaming intensified the noise in this otherwise quiet part of town. Every time another window opened and another woman screamed, Oinky squealed again. Pretty soon a few dogs had started barking too. Oinky looked down at the man lying in the rubbish, his eyes closed as the glow of red light lit up his stubbly face. He sniffed at the red liquid splattered around his head, it smelled of tomatoes. Oinky liked tomatoes so he licked at the liquid with his tongue, some of it dribbling from his spiky teeth and down his chin. The first woman screamed louder.

"Là, c'est un animal dangereux!" yelled an older woman, pulling on a golden threadbare dressing gown while the man she had been with headed for the door. Within a minute, while Oinky was lapping up the last of the sauce, the hue of red light changed to blue. Blue, red, blue, red. It was like being in a cheap nightclub, only without the music.

A few other men loomed into view in the alleyway, one by one slinking away. Oinky looked up at them, then up to the screaming women, then down the alleyway. Another man was creeping out through a doorway, still buttoning his shirt as he closed it quietly behind him. Beyond him, another man, this one wearing what looked like an upturned flowerpot on his head.

"Arrette!" called out the Gendarme, holding out something in front of him. The man stopped perfectly still. Women stopped screaming, instead holding their breath. The street was silent. Oink, said Oinky, as he considered his options. They didn't look good.

16

Meanwhile, in another similar street, Daisy walked warily, as though eyes were watching her. They were.

Stellios had been in Paris for over a year now. Since he had moved from Cyprus his life had never been better. Not long after he had arrived, he met Aggie, who worked in a massage parlour. Very soon, Stellios had persuaded her that she needed a manager, someone to look after her and her business needs. She had agreed and, for a sizable percentage of her earnings, he had stood in doorways and made contact with potential clients, sending them in her direction. Within a few weeks, Aggie's sister had come to visit, from wherever it is that they were from. Stellios had persuaded her that she needed a career in the big city, and very soon he was her manager too. From then, things had increased and he now had nine ladies of the night, all working for him, all giving him a percentage of their earnings. They had been easy to find, younger girls wandering the streets at night, lost, needing food and water, requiring a little guidance. Stellios didn't want to build a big enterprise, but ten, he thought, ten was a nice round number that would keep him with a decent income. He was watching his tenth employee now, although she didn't know it yet. Steady now, waiting his chance, he followed Daisy from the shadows. The poor girl was calling out something, calling out for someone, she sounded foreign. And she sounded desperate. It was best not to startle them, these girls were timid, afraid, naïve.

Little did Stellios know, Daisy was none of these things.

"Oinky!" she called, pushing at a pile of rubbish with her foot. The rubbish moved as two rats scurried out, one stopping to glare at her as though she did not belong here, this was not her territory. She was thinking the same thing, but Stellios wasn't. This was his territory, and if the girl wanted to be here, then she was welcome, as long as she paid. Red light from a high window lit up her pretty face, with those high cheekbones and that cheeky spiked hair. Yes this one would be ideal. She looked very young too, even better. As she neared the end of the dim alley, still calling out, the Greek pimp slipped down through a narrow gap and then appeared in front of her. Daisy screamed, but the man just gave her his best smile; a smile that he knew was irresistible.

"Let me help you?" he said, deciding to use English instead of French or Greek. Daisy eyed him suspiciously.

"Jeez, ya made me jump, so you did!"

The man smiled again, Irish, it just kept getting better. The punters just loved that Irish accent.

"It seems to me that you are looking for someone Miss...errr?"

"Daisy," said Daisy, then immediately wishing she hadn't.

"Well, Miss Daisy, I am a man who knows these streets very well. Who is it you have lost? Your mother? A brother? A small child perhaps? Hmmm?"

Daisy's mind whirred, something wasn't right about this man but she was tired and he seemed like he was trying to help. And he spoke English.

"A pig!" she replied.

"A pig?" repeated the young man, his greasy hair and even greasier leather jacket glistening under the glow of the street lamp.

Daisy suddenly realised how ridiculous this must have sounded.

"Yes, he is my pig. He ran away!"

Stellios raised his eyebrows. The usual scenario, probably a boyfriend she had a row with, and she called him a pig. It often happened like this.

"You want some coffee? Maybe a li'l drink of something?" He came a bit closer. "Maybe come back to my place? We can talk about it." There was something about his smile that first made her scared. "You wanna earn some money?" Daisy glanced down and saw the handle of a knife sticking out from Stellios' inside pocket. "Nice girl like you. You may get lost on these streets, eh?" His face moved nearer to hers and she smelt his awful breath, chilli and alcohol. A tingling sensation of fear ran down her arm as the man touched it with his leather gloved hand. A leather glove with the fingers missing. "I can look after you. Help you find your friend. If your pig-like friend comes around I can deal with him for you, you know, do a number on him. Did he hurt you baby? I'll hurt him back, you know what I'm saying?" Stellios opened his jacket to show off the knife that she had already noticed. Daisy's mind raced. The thought of this horrible creature 'dealing' with Oinky was too much for her.

"You get away from me, you hear? I've got good friends to protect me."

"Good friends? Ha! Good friends like your pigfaced-friend who allows you to wonder the streets at night?" Stellios made a show of looking around, putting his gloved hands above his eyes for effect. "Hello?" he called out.

110

"Hello?" shaking his head. "I don't see your friends now. I don't see your pig-like friends here to protect you. Do you?" Daisy didn't. "What I see is Stellios! He is here. Stellios will look after you. Pretty girl like you, needs someone like me, eh?" When he came back closer to Daisy, she was ready this time, turning to face him. Stellios put one hand behind her head, fingering her soft hair, pulling her towards him. She even puckered her lips, ready for his kiss before her right knee jerked upwards making a solid connection between the greasy man's legs.

"Arrrrggghhh!" said Stellios. RUN said Daisy's brain. Run went Daisy's legs, out into the alleyway, turning right, sprinting for all she was worth. Then there were footsteps behind her, leather boots on the solid pavement. Swearing. At least she guessed it was swearing, in French, or possibly Greek. Another block passed, then another as she ran, deeper into the city. People watched her go, seeing the man following her but making no attempt to help. After nearly five minutes Daisy slowed, leaning on a waste bin to get her breath back. Through the sound of her own panting she listened for the chasing footsteps, but they she couldn't hear them. Instead she heard the comforting sound of a police siren, or was it an ambulance, they all sounded the same? The sound was nearby; in fact, she could see blue lights flashing up ahead. People were shouting and she gathered herself up enough to take an interest, despite her own recent ordeal. Women were shouting, men were shouting, but Daisy didn't understand the words. One of the shouts was more of a high pitched squeal, echoing out into the night. A squeal she knew, a squeal she had been looking for. Daisy started to run once more, this time heading towards the blue lights. She was within a couple of blocks when she heard another sound, this one crackling out an echo around the solid brick walls. A single sound. Crack. And then silence.

By the time Daisy reached the scene, the street was empty except for a woman shouting down from an upstairs window, her pale breasts flashing out from under an old dressing gown, cigarette in her mouth. At the far end, a police van was just leaving, its siren blaring once again as she ran up towards it to see the vehicle disappear into the distance. Piles of rubbish lay scattered around the street, cardboard boxes, papers, a bin turned on its side. And blood. Some of it splattered around amongst the rubbish, some on the bin and a trail of it right the way up the street towards where the police van had been.

Above her, the woman was calling out, waving her arms at the mess. "C'est un animal dangereux! C'est un animal dangereux!" Making her way to the top end of the street, Daisy's heart sank. She sat on a water hydrant, put her head down in her hands and, for the first time in a good few years, started to cry. The woman was still shouting out, "c'est un animal dangereux!" and her temper rose up, pushing back the tears.

"He WASN'T dangerous, he was a poor defenceless creature!"

17

Meanwhile, in the back of a very fast moving vehicle, a poor defenceless creature lay very still. The reason he was still is not what you think.

The reason Oinky lay very still is that he was tangled up in a rope-net which fastened all his legs together. The more he had tried to struggle, the more it held him, until eventually he had given up, just lying still, terrified.

Out in the street, when the spotlight shone on him, Oinky had decided to run. He had known about running, it was his specialist subject. Squealing for all he was worth, which is possibly not very much, Oinky took to his hooves. But he hadn't got far when the gunshot sounded out, a bullet ricocheting of the wall near his head. Oinky had stopped in his tracks. Yes, out on the race-track, the gunshot had signalled the start of the race, but there, in that Parisian street it had scared him senseless. His legs had refused to carry him any further and, scared of another shot being fired, Oinky had just given up and laid down on the ground oinking. When the policeman had thrown the net over him, he had considered another gallant attempt at a getaway and that is when everything got all tangled up. Here he was now, wrapped in a strong net, heading who knows where?

Back on the street, Le Rue de R'marks, Daisy was thinking the same thing. Of heading who knows where? She may as well get back to the hotel, make the most of that comfortable bed, sleep on her decisions, and then in the morning she would make a plan and make her move. Little did she notice, in the shadows behind her, someone else was about to make theirs!

For the past half an hour, Stellios couldn't stop thinking about the young Irish girl. Yes he had Aggie, but he didn't fancy her any more, just used her to make money. But this girl was different, this Miss Daisy. Stellios wasn't as fit as he used to be and after five minutes of chasing, he had to stop, reaching into his pocket and pulling out a small pill. It was his last one but he could get more, he was Stellios, he could get whatever he wanted. As the drug had started to take effect, he too had heard the police siren. Something in his drug-filled Greek mind had made the connection between police and pigs, wasn't PIG a slang word that the English used for the police? Maybe that was who the girl had been looking for? Stellios had followed the sound of the siren and the blue flashing lights, staying in the shadows, wary, not wanting any contact with the Gendarmes. And then he had seen her, the girl, his new girl, sitting crying, looking lost and helpless. Fate was on his side.

Stellios didn't think Daisy would come quietly with him. In fact she had been rather violent last time, but he liked that, it showed a bit of spirit. A bit of Irish spirit! Clutching the handle of his knife, he took a deep breath and then stepped silently out of the shadows behind the girl, his strong arm pulling around her throat, locking it tight as he spoke.

"Well, Miss Daisy, we meet again. I told you that you needed help, and you did, huh? Were you running to tell the police? Going to report me to your pig friends? Well let me tell you, Miss Daisy, they won't bother me, they won't catch Stellios." Daisy struggled, trying to swing her arms into the man behind her until she felt the cold steel blade touch her throat. "So whada-you-say, Miss Daisy? You wanna come with Stellios, eh?" He drew a deep breath, taking in Daisy's scent, his mouth close to her ear. "What do you say, Miss Daisy," he repeated, "shall we go and have that drink now? Talk about things?" His grip tightened for a second, almost cutting off Daisy's breathing altogether. Feeling his hot breath on her neck, she nodded her head slightly, fear running through her veins like boiling water. Stellios loosened his grip again. "That's my girl!"

Reluctantly, Daisy got to her feet as the Greek roughly gripped her arm. "No funny stuff, you hear? There ain't nowhere to hide in this town, not without Stellios finding ya!" The man grinned as Daisy cursed her own stupidity. She had been so concerned that she might find Oinky that she had forgotten about the danger she had been running from until it had caught up with her again. Daisy didn't know exactly what this evil man wanted, but she suspected it wouldn't be what she wanted. As they stepped slowly back down the street, she looked down at the blood once more, tears coming back to her eyes. Was that it? Was the little pig finished? He would be no match for the police and their shoot-to-kill ideas. She wished they were here now.

Looking down at the ground, Daisy didn't notice a woman watching them from the upstairs windows, this time hiding back a little, out of view behind the curtains. Marionette may have been a lady of the night with perhaps a dubious career record, but you didn't do her line of work without knowing trouble when you saw it. And this foreign looking grease-ball in the leather jacket was trouble, Marionette was certain of that. As they passed, the woman was already reaching for the phone and dialling the Gendarmes for the second time in as many hours.

The discussion she had with the rude police officer on the phone did not go well. Marionette had little time for the police, in her line of work they were all about harassment and petty arrests. They were also, often, looking for other favours.

"Yes, I know this is the second time I have called. What?" she listened to the other end. "But it *was* a dangerous animal, I saw it attack that man. What?" Listening again. "Well, pig, wolf, bear, what's the difference, it was a *wild* creature and it *looked* evil!" Marionette fumbled with her cigarette lighter, inhaling a breath of smoke and then blowing it out into the air. "But I am telling you, this man is evil too." She described Stellios. "And I know evil when I see it and you need to get your sorry arse (the words 'desolet derrière' sounds so much more polite in French!) down here to Rue de R'marks, pronto! ...Allo? Allo?" The line had gone dead. Marionette replaced the receiver and looked out of the window again. The couple had gone. She sighed. Oh well, she had tried.

Back at the Gendarmerie, the duty sergeant was having trouble getting himself heard when he tried to report the call he had just received. He had trouble getting himself heard because of the incredible noise from one small but highly audible pig. It didn't *look* evil, but possibly a bit *wild*. Untangling a thrashing screaming small pig from a rope-net is not a job to be taken lightly and far more of a challenge that say, speaking to the duty sergeant. For example, at least the duty sergeant didn't have razor sharp teeth that tried to bite your fingers off. The two officers stepped outside so they could be heard.

"Sounds like Stellios," nodded the Officer Tabelle.

"You think we should check it out?"

The Officer sighed. "I suppose so. I will go, you can deal with that creature in there!"

"What should we do with it?"

"Sort it out and then chuck it in the cells, I guess. Maybe we can have it for lunch?" Officer Tabelle climbed on to the saddle of his motorcycle, pulling a glove over his bleeding finger and kicking its engine into life while the duty sergeant went down to the kitchens to fetch a sharp knife.

Daisy was feeling a sharp knife too, the point of it sticking into her back, after she had tried to escape. Stellios was not quite so happy now, and the effect of the drugs was starting to wear off. This girl had spat at him, tried to escape, even swore at him as he gave her his best sweet talk. She looked so innocent too, with her flush cheeks and spiky hair, but he suspected under that exterior was a wild animal. He had seen flashes of it in those fiery green eyes. Stellios was quite looking forward to taming this animal.

The same could be said for the duty officer at Paris Gendarmerie.

Stellios and Daisy reached a doorway and he did his best to dig into his pocket for his keys while holding the girl and the knife. A blue light flashed, faintly at first and then getting more intense towards the top end of this narrow dark street. Gendarmes again. What now? As he fumbled with the key in the lock, Daisy took her chance, thrashing her ram around and knocking the keys from his hand. Stellios lashed out, the silver blade catching her across the arm. Screaming, she ran out into the darkness, the blue glow lighting her only way as she headed towards it. Tabelle raised his gun, first training it on her and then on to a shadow in the darkness. Stellios had seen the gun just in time and scurried away around the corner, sprinting away from his would-be captor. From around the street corner, another officer shouted, a shot fired, followed by a scream as Tabelle turned back to the girl, sensing she was hurt. Daisy was leaning against the wall near to the police motorbike by the time he returned, clutching her arm which was dripping blood.

"Did you get him," she asked, breathlessly, in her Irish brogue.

"Oui mademoiselle, I zink zo!" he said, trying his best English. "P'raps you need to go to 'ospital?" He was looking at the slowly dripping blood.

"You too?" said Daisy, giving him a faint smile. They both looked down to the officer's finger, which was also dripping blood. "Zis? Oh zis is nothing. Just an animal bite! A very wild animal!"

18

By the time Daisy reached the police station, she was feeling extremely weary. Outside the sun was starting to rise; it had been a long night. Officer Tabelle had turned out to be quite a nice man, as the two of them sat and chatted, waiting to be stitched up at Charles de Gaule hospital in central Paris. Now, with matching bandages, they walked through the double doors, Tabelle nodding to the duty sergeant.

Daisy had told the officer all about Oinky and how he was lost, and the man had radioed in to let the station know that they had found the pig's owner. She was elated to know he was still alive, and safe. OK, Daisy was not rightfully the pig's owner, and in fact Daisy had no longer been her name. 'IMELDA MORRIS' she wrote, struggling to form the letters on the white paper form at the desk, address: The Farm, Weston-on-the-mere, England. "It's by the sea!" she said, as means of an explanation for the exceptionally long town name, smiling as she told her little lie. Tabelle had already filled out a statement, all in French, based on what she had told him about Stellios. She signed her name at the bottom.

BRUNO. That was the name on the blue plastic bowl on the floor in front of Oinky. It was empty, where it had been full. Three faces peered in at him through the glass as the pig oinked quietly in his sleep.

"I deeed not know what to geeeve im," the sergeant was saying, "zo eee ad the cassoulet!"

"The cassoulet?" remarked officer Tabelle, "zat was for me!"

The duty officer gave a Parisian shrug. "C'est la vie, mon ami!"

Oinky woke with a start when the door opened, jumping up and diving under the single piece of furniture in the police cell, a bed against the wall. His mind raced back to events from earlier, of being trapped, surrounded, arrested and captured. He remembered a man with a knife, Oinky always remembered men with knives and that man was standing in the doorway now. Oink, he said loudly, mainly to himself. Then he noticed the empty bowl on the floor, at least the man had brought him some dinner, some nice stew with beans in it.

"Oinky?" said a voice, a calm and enticing voice. "Oinky, grub!" Brains were not Oinky's greatest possession, but a good sense of smell was right up there with full-speed-ahead when it came to pig senses. His snout twitched as a familiar aroma filled the little cell. Oink.

"Oinky, I have brought you something," said the girl's voice again. Her feet appeared next to the bed and Oinky considered biting them and running away. But she did sound kind, and familiar. And she smelled nice. Well, something smelled nice. He poked his head out and looked up into Daisy's green eyes with a sense of recognition.

"Oinky, it's me, Daisy. I mean Imelda," she corrected herself, as the two officers watched from the open doorway. "Look, I have brought you something." Daisy held out a cream-cracker towards the trembling pig. Oink.

At first Oinky had taken exception to the collar around his neck. It had taken Daisy nearly a whole packet of biscuits to persuade him that she wasn't trying to hurt him, but she had been very patient. When the lead was attached,

120

he pulled very hard, dragging her along with it as she clung to the bed for support. Two policemen standing in the doorway guffawed with laughter at first, until Daisy gave them a fearful glare.

Now he waited patiently in the reception of the police station, as Daisy signed the release form; released without charge.

"Au-revoir, Imelda! Au-revoir, OONKY!" called out the duty sergeant. Officer Tabelle gave Daisy a kiss on both cheeks, telling her to be careful out there and the two of them stepped out into the Parisian dawn at around 5am, girl and pig as one.

"Look, Oinky!" whispered Daisy, "the Eifel Tower. Isn't it wonderful?" Oinky looked up as Daisy crouched down beside him, pointing. He thought he recognised the word Trifle and oinked in approval as the two of them set off towards it, Daisy ignoring stares from passers by.

*   *   *   *   *

Fifi had been to the hairdressers again. Fifi wasn't keen on the hairdresser and even less keen on what the hairdresser had done this time. And all those stupid pop-poms? She trotted along the trottoir behind the housekeeper, out for her early morning walk; Fifi didn't particularly like the housekeeper either and was generally in a bad mood. Pink, why pink? It made her look like some kind of freak!

Oinky, on the other hand, was getting used to walking on his new lead, even quite enjoying it. That is until he saw a pink thing coming in the other direction. The pink thing saw him. "Bark, bark, yap, yap," it screamed at him, snapping its jaws like some kind of machine.

"Mon dur!" shouted the voluptuous housekeeper, her wide eyes staring at Oinky. "Fifi, arrette!" Fifi didn't arrette because she didn't know what this creature was, and she knew every dog around here. Was it a dog? "Bark, snap, bark!" Fifi attacked it with the ferocity of a werewolf, teeth sinking in to its flapping ear.

The attack had taken Oinky by surprise but somehow he hadn't been scared of this ridiculous looking creature and, for the first time in his life, he fought back. Both Fifi and Oinky had taken Daisy by surprise as she daydreamed her way along the pavement, periodically glancing up at the tower looming ahead. Squeal, bark, snap, bite, the mayhem erupted, a hullabaloo of noise spilling in through open windows into the sleeping houses. Before she knew it, there was blood, lots of it. And fur. A pink dog with sharp teeth had stopping barking, even stopped snapping, it was now yelping. An obese black lady wearing a headscarf was yelling, screaming in fact. Windows opened, more shouting. A timid pig with a mouthful of pink fur, a pool of blood, a yelping dog, at 5.30am, that is generally the sort of thing that makes people shout.

Yves Jubert rolled himself his first cigarette of the day, as he ambled along the path, taking a shortcut to work this morning. He liked to get in early so he could avoid the rush hour, his head still clear before the grind of daily scandal landed on his desk. Alerted by a sudden sound nearby, Yves couldn't believe his luck, approaching the live street-fight at a running pace. In all his ten years of working at Le Monde newspaper in Paris, the only thing he had ever witnessed on his way to work was a minor car crash. By the time he was within ten metres, his Nikon was already in his hand, firing off the first shot. Photo journalists don't really assess the situation, they take pictures first, then ask questions later. Snap, snap, snap went the camera, snap, snap, snap went the two pink animals. He had seen it all, caught it all right here in his trusty Nikon camera. Slinging it back over his shoulder, Yves now had his notebook and pencil ready, firing off questions into the screaming mele. "Housekeeper, attacked, wild animal," he scribbled in French. Daisy was rather stunned by it all when the man fired questions at her too, in rapid incomprehensible French.

"It attacked Oinky! That fierce dog attacked Oinky! He was just defending himself." Daisy pointed to the dog, now snuggled up in the arms of the large woman and looking sorry for itself. The reporter looked from pig to dog and back to pig, curls of pink fur still hanging from its mouth. He couldn't understand what she was saying, but that wouldn't stop Yves getting a story down in his little book. Oh boy, this was going to be a great story, maybe one that would get him promoted. The housekeeper told him, in French, that "...the dog belongs to Madam Rousel, the

Minister for Rural Affairs, and that the dog's name is Fifi. She had just been taking it for its early morning walk when the creature attacked. She didn't know what sort of creature it was, possibly a badger?"

At that very moment, wrapped in a very elegant dressing-gown, the Minister for Rural Affairs appeared in a doorway, fifty metres away. She looked, screamed and then ran in their direction. The creature, which was not a badger, decided that it was time to run away. Daisy had been considering the same notion when her mind was made up for her as her left arm nearly left its socket, so strong was the pull of the Oinky on his lead against the weakness of the injured arm. They crossed the road, burst through a hole in a privet hedge and disappeared into the park beyond. This hadn't looked good and now they were leaving the scene of the accident. Except that four local resident witnesses, a government minister and a hysterical housekeeper hadn't considered it to be an accident. To them it had been a crime, a cold blooded attack, unprovoked. Yes, for Yves Jubert, it would be a good day and if he hurried, he could make the second edition.

19

Pat MacGowan took his place at the breakfast table in the small but elaborate dining room in the Hotel de Ruffit, glancing round at one or two of the other clientele. Many of them averted his gaze, as though guilty of something. Ordering a coffee and breakfast from the well tailored waiter, Pat unfolded his complimentary copy of the newspaper which was tucked between the bread basket and water jug.

"Begorra, begosh, bejeazuz, to be sure!" blurted out the Irishman when he discovered the photograph on the front cover.

"Pardon Monsieur?" asked the waiter.

"Bejeazuz, tis Daisy!" replied Pat, pointing to the picture. The waiter nodded his head.

"Ah, Oui Monsieur, elle ne pas dans le chamber ce matin!"

"Speak English, will ya? I can't understand all that foreign rubbish," his voice was getting louder with rage. "And where the hell is she now?"

"That ees wurt I am telling you, Monsieur, the gurl ess not ere!"

"Not here? Well where in St Michaels name is she?"

The man raised his shoulders, opening the palms of his hands upwards, adding a patronising smile and a raise of the eyebrows, and said nothing.

For those of you unaware, this is known as a Parisian shrug, possibly one of the most infuriating things ever to come out of Paris since Napoleon!

Certainly Pat was furious when he looked back at the picture again, a black woman holding a scruffy dishevelled dog and a small pig with a mouthful of pink fur. He didn't need the headline translating, which as just as well, as the waiter had turned on his heel, uncertain if the Irishman was going to get violent.

"Where the heck is that girl? You wait till I get my hands on her!" yelled an irate six foot six Irishman as a waiter cowered in the kitchen.

That girl was thinking the same thing, she knew the incident would have made it into the papers, and she had a pretty good idea that Pat MacGowan wouldn't be too pleased about it. That is one reason why she was now heading for the train station instead of the hotel. Oinky had taken a lot of calming down, when she had eventually stopped him running. She had looked into his little eyes and told him everything was going to be alright, and that he hadn't done anything wrong.

"Good piggy, Oinky, you are a good piggy!" Oinky had oinked in agreement.

But before long, people were starting to recognise him, whispering to each other as they passed. You didn't see too many small pigs on a collar and lead, well not in Paris

126

anyway, but there was one on the front page of the daily newspaper matching Oinky's description. And he was WANTED!

Trying her best to ignore the stares, Daisy scanned the line of shops until she found one selling what she needed, a little bell ringing as the two of them entered. Needless to say, some screaming followed. They possibly didn't see many pigs in this baby-clothes shop either, so Daisy stepped back outside, tying Oinky's lead to the drainpipe on the street.

"Now you stay here, OK?" she said to him, sternly. Oinky oinked.

A woman passed by holding the hand of a small boy. "Oooh, Mama, regardez le petty chien!"

"Attention, c'est dangereaux!" screeched his mother, yanking him out of reach by his arm. All the other pedestrians in the street gave a wide birth to this animal tied to a drain-pipe, the one that may be 'dangereaux'. Some of them stopped and stared, one man pointed his phone at Oinky, snapping a photo. Oinky looked up at him with sad eyes. Oink.

Daisy wasn't long before she was back out of the shop, carrying a brown bag. Strutting up to Oinky, she untied his lead and walked away, scowling at the assembled crowd as though everything was perfectly normal. It won't be long, she thought, before the police arrive, or even worse, Pat MacGowan.

In a quiet corner of a smaller park, Oinky wriggled and twisted while the Irish girl did her best to cover him up with the clothes she had bought. Baby-grows were only made in one shape and that was, strangely enough, baby shape and not pig shaped, but eventually she managed to slide his twitching feet into the towelling garment, doing up the poppers under his stomach. The bonnet was a little more difficult, especially getting his ears to stay under the elastic. Now wrapped in a knitted white shawl, she gathered him up in both arms and headed for the ticket office.

"One adult and one baby," she demanded from the young woman behind the glass window, who eyed her dubiously. These girls got younger and younger, thought the woman, this one was surely too young to have a baby. And the poor thing, it didn't look well. Maybe she should call a doctor for them both?

Daisy couldn't stop her hand trembling as she gathered up the two tickets and her change from the counter, smiling sweetly to the woman.

"Merci" she said.

"Oink," said Oinky, peering out from under his bonnet.

"Bon voyage!" said the woman sadly. They're probably running away, she thought.

They were indeed running away, but where to? Their destination had been a random decision from Daisy, and Oinky hadn't had much say in the matter. She looked down at her ticket as the pig sat quietly on her lap. St Tropez was the only place that she had vaguely heard of out of the list of destinations on the vast sign up on the wall, the one that kept changing every few seconds. She was pretty sure it was near the ocean and she loved the ocean. Daisy pronounced the name quietly to herself. San-trop-ay, that was how the woman had pronounced it. Grand Central station was very busy, people striding backwards and forwards, men with briefcases, woman with children, everyone seemed to know where they were going. Thankfully nobody took much notice of a young girl and her baby, sitting on the metal bench patiently, as she watched the clock ticking away on

128

the wall. Ten more minutes, that's all. She looked around at the great building, with its intricate metalwork, painted red and gold, supporting the bright glass roof. There must have been a dozen platforms, far bigger than any station she had visited before, but then she had never done much train travel, just a trip up to Belfast once, to visit an uncle for Christmas. Daisy found herself whispering to her travelling companion.

"Look, isn't it so grand," she told him, "but so busy? I never want to live in a place this busy, do you?" Oinky didn't, his little eyes scanning the passers by, always wary. Oink, he said.

Despite her sitting in the middle of the bench, a mother with two small children approached them, the mother looking weary and dragging a heavy suitcase. The children weren't weary, far from it, they were extremely excited.

"Harry! Rebecca! Sit there and wait patiently!" said their mother sternly, in perfect English. "The train will be here in ten minutes. Miss, do you mind if we sit?" Daisy did mind, she minded a lot, but it was also comforting to hear an English voice. Nodding her head, she forced a smile and shuffled along the bench, Harry taking the seat next to her and his sister beside him. Daisy turned her face away from them, pulling the shawl high up over Oinky's face so he couldn't be seen. Nine minutes now, just nine minutes.

"Now sit there and behave while I go and make a phone call," commanded the woman in English, although her accent hinted of foreign origins. The two children sat there behaving, as the woman strode off, a bit more forcefully now she wasn't dragging the suitcase.

Rebecca was the first to speak, as soon as the woman was out of earshot. "We're going on holiday!" she said excitedly to Daisy, who had decided not to let on that she spoke English. She smiled at the child and then looked away, hoping it would deter her. It didn't. "Can I look at your baby?"

Daisy had to think fast, she didn't want this child inspecting the baby, so she chose to ignore the question. But Rebecca persevered, as do all inquisitive children, tugging at Daisy's sweatshirt. "Can I see your baby?"

"Oink!"

Rebecca giggled, Harry giggled too. "Do you speak English?"

"Oink!" Daisy tightened her grip on Oinky, trying to keep him quiet.

"That didn't sound like English, Becky," Harry told her. "I think it's German. Are you German?" Daisy thought about this and then nodded, desperately hoping Harry didn't speak German. He did.

"Können wir Ihr Baby bitte betrachten?" Daisy was trapped. She shook her head at the boy. "Oh!" he said, somewhat dejectedly.

"Oink," said Oinky.

"Germans are funny people," Harry told his sister quietly. "Can you smell something funny?" Rebecca nodded that she cold smell something funny. Daisy could smell it too.

"Oink!" said Oinky, the perpetrator of the offending smell.

"Pooey!" said Rebecca and Harry at once, holding their nose.

Changing a baby in Grande Central station in Paris is no easy task. Changing a baby when you have never changed a baby before is no simple exercise either. Changing a small reluctant pig in Grand Central station

130

could be determined as nothing less than challenging. Daisy tried to stay calm as she headed for the toilets, with only 7 minutes to go before her train departed, with an unfortunate smell following her.

In the little room that had a picture of a mother and baby on the door, some squealing could be heard, interspersed with plenty of oinking, as Daisy battled with the task. It wasn't nice, having to rinse the baby-grow under the hot tap with one hand while trying to hold down an unwilling pig with the other. Oinky didn't like it either.

Outside the door, near the washbasins, some other people were also none too keen on the noise and one rather caring old lady thought it best if she alerted the guards.

"Allo, êtes-vous bien dedans là?" sounded a voice, knocking on the door very loudly. The knocking and shouting alarmed Oinky, who squealed even louder.

"She wont understand you, she's German," said a young girl's voice. "I will fetch my mother, she speaks German." Footsteps trotted off while more people spoke to each other outside the door. Daisy couldn't understand what they were saying and she could barely hear them above the noise coming from the near hysterical pig. It is possible they were complaining about the smell.

"Oinky, it's alright," she whispered and then repeated it, louder in case he hadn't heard.

"Oinky? Qui est Oinky?" muttered the guard outside. At last the pig quietened down a little, and stopped wriggling enough for her to put his clothes back on. This really wasn't working but all she could think of was getting on that train and getting out of here. A train revved its giant engine, rattling the walls of the little cubicle, sending a tremor through the entire building.

Helga Hardwick, or Frauline Helga as the children called her, was not a woman to be messed with. Years of teaching adolescents had toughened her already armoured personality to a level which matched her physical strength, the power of which was now being used on the door outside.

"Sind Sie gut?" she demanded in a haughty tone. Daisy thought the door was going to come off its hinges and the noise started Oinky squealing again, that and the roaring train. She would have to open it.

"Oi am foine!" she called back in her native Irish brogue.

"Oi am foine?" repeated the German ogre, "what sort of language is that? That's not German? Sounds more Russian to me? I thought you said she was German?"

"Well, Harry said she was!" complained Rebecca.

"Do you believe everything that Harry says, child?" scolded Helga, "if he told you the moon was made of cheese, would you believe him?"

"No, Mother!"

"Well, don't just stand there, you useless woman, go and find a Russian translator." Helga was now instructing the guard, who looked at her blankly, having no idea what she was saying. The guard retaliated in a flurry of French which sounded quite aggressive; you didn't get to be a female guard in Paris without showing a little aggression. More footsteps outside, more revving of engines. Daisy made sure Oinky was fully covered up and quietly unlatched the door. When she looked through a tiny gap, the obese German woman and the French female guard were having a stand-off, both shouting at each other in different languages. Complete with the temporarily silent Oinky hidden under his blanket, she made a dash for the exit, not stopping to look round. Out in the station foyer once more, Daisy ran towards platform seven, where the sound of the train's engine was coming from, a uniformed guard blowing his whistle.

"Allez, mademoiselle!" he shouted to her as she made her way up the step and through the doorway into the train, just before it closed behind her with a swishing sound. Thankfully the carriage was reasonably empty and she found a seat facing a table. Outside the window, to her horror, the fat German woman with her two children were struggling down the platform, towing the oversized suitcase. It was impossible to hear what she was saying to the uniformed guard, but it certainly looked like she was demanding something. The man pointed down towards the front of the train and made a waving motion, as if to tell her to hurry, while Daisy kept her head down low and out of sight. It was just her luck that the woman was travelling on the same train as her, but at least she had escaped from the guard. Nervously she waited for the train to move, so that she could escape from Paris altogether.

20

"Ticket?" said the guard, holding out his hand.

"Oink," said Oinky, as Daisy fumbled in her bag for it. The guard eyed Oinky suspiciously as he hid under his blanket, before taking the tickets and inspecting them, clipping the corners with his special pliers. "A quelle age c'est l'enfant?" he asked, "ow, old?"

"Ten months!" She lied, holding up 10 fingers. While her hands were free, Oinky wriggled under his blanket, the tip of his nose poking out.

"Oink!" The guard jumped back, dropping the tickets on the table. He had never seen such an ugly child, its face was all deformed. And it grunted? His eyes changed from suspicion to sympathy. This poor girl, having to cope with such problems, it was a shame for her. Once he had completed his inspection of all the passengers, he would make a point of coming back to talk to her. Maybe he could bring Natalie, she spoke a little English. The guard smiled at her and moved on.

"Haven't I told you to stay still when people speak to us?" she said, scolding Oinky but smiling too, peeling back the blanket again. There was nobody around up this end of the carriage, so she removed the blanket once the guard was out of sight. Oinky sat on the comfortable chair, looking out of the window as the countryside sped by at nearly 200 miles per hour.

"We're off to the seaside," she said to him, as though holding a conversation with a friend. "Won't that be nice?"

Oinky didn't know what the seaside was. In fact, he wasn't too sure what was happening at all, as he tried to look at things as they passed. It made him dizzy so he stopped and looked at Daisy instead. This girl seemed very nice. Yes she had tried to make him wear those silly clothes and had nearly strangled him when he had done a pooh, but he thought she was kind and he liked her and, most important of all, at least she didn't attack him with knives. She also gave him biscuits and, while she tried to read a magazine she had found in the rack by the door, Oinky went in search of some in her bag.

"Hey, stop that!" she said, but he wasn't listening. Expectantly he nuzzled his nose into the bag; they had to be in there somewhere?

Daisy didn't really go in for fashion, Gucci and Louis Vuitton were for other girls; her bag was more of a draw-string type that younger girls would use for, say, gym shoes. She didn't have a great deal of worldly possessions, and the clothes that she had accumulated were now still back at the hotel. So, in this bag was a hairbrush, some hair-gel and a few other things that girls carry around with them, often for no particular reason. Oinky sniffed them all, in his quest to find some of those nice cream-crackers as the girl tried to snatch the bag back. And there were some, he found them nestling at the bottom.

"Oinky, give it back!" Oinky wasn't going to give it back, not until he had eaten his booty, so he jumped down off the seat and went under the little table, still with the bag over his head. Daisy's smile dropped from her face as she tried to pull him back, but she didn't have his lead. In fact he had his lead, it was in the bag.

"Oinky, will you get back here!"

Out into the aisle strutted a small pig.

Gilles, the train guard was on his way back, along with Natalie, to comfort the young woman with the poor deformed baby. However, as he arrived through the door into the carriage, the poor deformed baby was heading towards them wearing blue pyjamas, with a sinister black bag over its head. From inside the bag could be heard the sound of crunching biscuits and satisfactory oinking.

"Oh, mon dieu!" said the two guards, in perfect harmony.

"Oh my god!" said Daisy, round about the same time.

"Oink!" said the poor deformed baby, who was actually, for once, a reasonably happy pig. That state of happiness didn't last too long when, as often occurs when a small happy pig trots down the aisle of a fast moving train, people started screaming.

"Everybody stay calm, he is harmless," were not really words that many French people understood. Fortunately, Natalie did.

Natalie Beroche had been brought up on a farm in Normandy, and on that farm they had some pigs. (ee-i-ee-i-o etc*). So, while a very confused guard called Gilles thought he saw a small deformed baby running on all fours, so ugly it had to have its head covered with a sack, Natalie saw the pig for what it was. A pig in blue pyjamas admittedly, but definitely a pig! The pig, on the other hand, didn't see Natalie. In fact it couldn't see anything, so dark was it inside the sinister black sack and, now there were people shouting, it ran for all it was worth.

Between each carriage on high speed trains, there is a sliding door which is, as I am sure you are aware, opened by pushing by a button. After a short period of time, the sliding door closes, automatically. Gilles and Natalie, unable to stop the now squealing creature, stepped aside, just as the door behind them closed. From then on the squealing got much louder, in fact it intensified so much, now that Oinky was trapped halfway between two carriages by a sliding door, that it could be heard by the driver, three carriages further down.

Oinky really believed this was the end, as he struggled to break free of this creature that was gripping him so tightly and, as is normal in these situations, his fear gave rise to a rather natural, albeit unbearable, smell. The smell filled the carriage behind him at about the same rate that the sound filled the ones in front of him. It was probably a toss of a coin as to which end was the most unpleasant. Quickly seeing the situation, Daisy tried to run towards the door in order to hit the button to open it, but was severely hindered by all the rest of the passengers running the other way, a guard included. The only person staying anywhere near the pig was Natalie who eyed Daisy with suspicion and was just about to tell her that farm animals were definitely not allowed on the high speed train. She never got the chance because the driver, who was convinced he heard screaming back there, had taken a rather rash decision and hit the emergency brake.

INERTIA is a word sometimes used in physics lessons, and maybe what happened next should be included in that lesson. People who had, until very recently, been heading away from the screaming pig, now found themselves heading towards it once more as the train slowed down from 200 miles per hour to zero, very, very, quickly, its wheels now making a screeching sound which harmonised quite nicely with a squealing pig. Not just people either, just about everything in the carriage continued on its journey while the vehicle slowed down; cups of coffee, luggage, a very smart ladies hat, it all shot forward due to gravitational forces beyond its control. In fact, the only thing that didn't shoot forward was the pig itself, which was still held fast by the double doors gripping its ribs. That is until Daisy who, remember, was on a mission to hit the release button, succeed in her task.

If you have ever been to a circus, I hope you have been lucky enough to witness that great trick they do where they fire a human into the air out of a cannon. If you haven't, please try and imagine what it would be like. Then, replace 'human' with 'small pig' and 'cannon' with 'sliding doors', and you may get a picture of the impending scene. Oinky shot forward at approximately 80 miles per hour, possibly breaking the land-speed record for pigs in the process, with his feet barely touching the ground. Down the next carriage he went, complete with pyjamas, as the aisle became a human bowling alley, with the ball being made up of squeal and pinkness. One by one passengers were up-ended as the ball kept on going, taking them out at the knees. Through the carriage, into the next carriage and the one beyond went Oinky, gathering a few quite fashionable articles of clothing en route, until he eventually arrived at the door to the drivers cab. Which was open.

Drivers of high speed trains get to witness many things during the course of their work, not all of them pleasant. The driver of this train was having an unpleasant experience which had caused him to jump out from his seat and head into the toilet. However, it was the driver of a train passing from the other direction that was to witness something that he could really spin into a tale to tell his grand-children, as he tooted his whistle. What he saw was barely credible but, as he later told the newspapers, it had to be true because he saw it with his own eyes. He also passed the breathalyser test.

What he saw was a pig, in blue pyjamas, wearing a ladies hat with a turquoise feather, (he was very specific about the colour), driving the 9.15 Paris to St Tropez train!

21

Daisy stepped down from the carriage on to the platform, amidst glares from quite a few passengers and train staff, with her pet pig following behind her on a lead. Oinky no longer wore his baby-grow suit, his cover had been blown and anyway, much of it was now ripped and torn after sliding a couple of hundred metres on his bum. No, the clothes were in the bin and Daisy and her animal had been asked to leave the train at the next stop. Her now having done so, the entire train heaved a sigh of relief as an almost acceptable level of normality was restored.

Oinky looked up at the great sign saying TOULOUSE.

"Oink!" he said.

"Oh, bummer!" said Daisy, scanning the tree lined streets and coming to terms with the fact that Toulouse was not actually by the sea. As she strolled along, they passed a café and she went to sit down and order a coffee.

"Non, Madomoselle, par de cochon!" No swine allowed. She moved on to another and then another, continually getting the same answer.

"But he is my pet," she argued, wearily. By lunchtime Daisy was close to tears, feeling like Mary and Joseph, with no room at the inn for baby Jesus. Baby Jesus, alias Oinky Grub, wasn't too impressed either and he was hungry. Her aimless walking had led the two of them out into the main square of the town and, as with many French cities, this was a rather large square which housed a daily market. Rows and rows of market stalls appeared as if from nowhere, selling just about anything edible a person, or pig, could wish for. Brightening up considerably, the two of them investigated what was on offer at the very first stall, Daisy from what was on the table, Oinky from what was underneath it. And what was under it was a vegetables.

"Allors!! Allez-zee," called out the frowning stall-holder as Oinky helped himself from a box of carrots. Daisy yanked Oinky back by his lead and looked at the large French woman apologetically.

"I am sorry, he is not very well trained, and we have had a difficult journey." The woman eyed the pair of them suspiciously, then bent down behind her stall and produced a loaf of stale bread, a smile spreading across her rosy-cheeked face. Oinky wasn't able to smile on account of his being a pig, but if he had been another animal, say a human for instance, he certainly would have done. Lying down under the green plastic sheet that covered the table, he held the French loaf between his front feet and tucked in.

Above the table Daisy smiled too. "Merci, buckups!" she said, listening to the contented sounds coming from Oinky. She scanned the wares spread out on the table, licking her lips. In front of her were sausage rolls and pastries as well as an array of fresh vegetables and fruit. Tempted as she was to the sausage rolls, she felt it may be a bit callous of her to eat one now she had a pet pig, so she chose a selection of other things, pointing to each one in turn as the lady put them in a brown paper bag.

Daisy paid the woman and dragged Oinky towards a metal bench, the pig still clutching half the loaf in his jaws. As she sat and ate her croissant followed by some kind of cheese sandwich, she noticed quite a few of the stall holders watching her with interest. Oinky finished his bread loaf in record speed and then she fed him the crusts of her sandwich which he also gobbled down.

"Oh Jeez," sighed the girl to herself, "what are we supposed to do now, Oinky?" Oinky didn't know the answer to this one but, having finished his lunch, he was still a bit peckish. He smelled an odour drifting towards him, something he hadn't smelled before. It was coming from one of the market stalls further down the row.

"Oink. Oink," he said, tugging at the lead.

"What's up, Oinky?" Daisy got to her feet as the pig dragged her across the tarmac square towards the market stall. A man stood behind it and smiled as they approached.

"Bonjour, Mademoiselle," he beamed, his kind eyes shining at her through thick glasses. "C'est un bon cochon!"

"Er, hello," said the girl suspiciously, "I am sorry, I don't understand what you're saying." She was about to move on but Oinky pulled her closer to the stall, his nose twitching up towards the table.

142

"Ah, you speak English," said the man, still grinning. Daisy's mood lightened a little when the man spoke, glad to hear a familiar language. She looked at his stall for the first time. On one side were some small twigs sticking out of soil pots, about 20 centremetres long. It was the other end of the table that Oinky had been more interested in, where there was a wicker basket containing some kind of mushrooms. He wasn't just interested, he was now going frantic as he tried to jump up at the table to reach them. The man held out has hand for the girl to shake.

"Richard Pyle," he said, his voice upper class English, "call me Dick."

"Hello," she replied, not willing to give her name until she had worked out who she was going to be this time. "Oinky, will you stop that!"

"He's got a great nose," said Dick, pulling the basket a little further out of the pig's reach.

"What *are* those things?" Daisy looked up at the sign over the stall for the first time, trying to read the long word. Dick beat her to it.

"Truffles!" he said, "Truffle-tree dot com!"

Neither Daisy nor Oinky had any idea what a truffle was but, unlike Daisy who thought they looked horrible, Oinky just knew they were the finest smelling thing he had ever encountered.

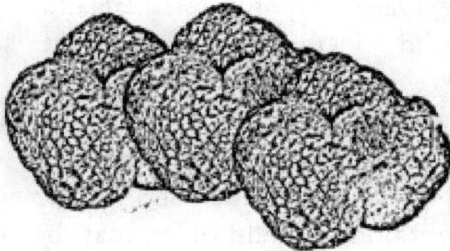

"Care to try a little bit?" Dick cut a tiny square from one of the mushrooms and held it out towards her. She took it from him and held it up to her nose before licking the corner of it.

"Euch!" she exclaimed, passing it back to the man but he shook his head.

"Give it to your friend, I bet he will like it."

Like it? Oinky thought it was the finest food he had ever tasted, twice as nice as cream-crackers and they were his favourite up until then. Come to think of it, cream-crackers and tasty mushroom would have been the finest meal he could ever imagine.

"Pigs love them, and so do most humans. Have you any idea how much these things are worth?" Daisy didn't, but considered a few pennies would be plenty for the smelly things. "Three thousand pounds a kilo!" Dick let the words hang in the air for a few seconds, watching the reaction on the girl's face as her jaw dropped open.

"How much?"

Dick repeated the figure. "That's what the top chefs have to pay. We just sell them wholesale. Would you like a cup of tea?" Daisy didn't know what she wanted, as Oinky pulled hard on the lead try to get some more truffles.

"Err, thanks."

"And you are?"

"Daisy, Daisy May. I'm from Ireland."

"Splendid. I thought I detected some brogue. Sugar?"

She shook her head as he poured the brown tea into a plastic mug from a silver thermos flask.

"PG Tips," he continued and then lowered his voice, as if the neighbouring stall-holder may be listening. "I've been in this country ten years and I still can't drink French tea, it's like dish-water. Sit." Daisy sat on the folding chair that she was offered. "Now, do tell?"

22

Within the hour, Daisy was looking across at this stranger with his rolled-up sleeves and scruffy appearance in the front of his small rattling van, wondering about the decision she had made. Dick seemed like an honest man, as far as she could tell, so she had told him her full story. He had listened and laughed when she mentioned the racing-pig show. "Your man Pat sounds like a right entrepreneur," he chuckled, "it sounds like the sort of thing I would do."

Then he told her exactly what he did do and then she had viewed him with renewed admiration. So much so, that when he offered to take her home to his place and put her up for a few days, she hadn't hesitated. He had seemed to like Oinky too and Oinky certainly had liked him.

The pig lay on the floor by her feet, snoring. It had been a long journey for both of them and after Oinky had eaten a second loaf of stale bread, he felt that a little nap was in order. He dreamed of tasty mushrooms.

Fields of bright yellow sunflowers came in and out of view as the beautiful French countryside whizzed past the window outside. Inside, Dick continued telling the story of how he came to be a Truffle magnate, as he drove on at break-neck speeds.

The man had been in business in the city of London for many years, with a vested interest in the restaurant trade. Ten years ago, like many other British people, Dick had taken a decision to move out from the city and bought a small farm in the Gascony region of France to enjoy a quieter lifestyle. Again, like many other British people, he had then started thinking of ways to make a little extra money to support this lifestyle without the need for a proper job. The idea of truffles had come to him in when he had experienced the outrageous price that he had to pay in one of his London restaurants.

To finance the start of Dick's truffle operation, he had sold the baby oak trees to members of the public, over the internet. And the money had flooded in, as many people bought into the idea of owning their own oak tree in France, with the prospect of producing a healthy profit from the sale of truffles. Within a couple of years, he had over a thousand trees growing, all being paid for by other people. The whole idea was quite ingenious. Many of the tree owners like to visit the farm each year, some of them slightly disappointed that, in the first few years at least, their precious tree was no more than just a twig. All good things come to those who wait, Dick told them, while he charged them handsomely for bed & breakfast.

They rounded a sharp corner and he swerved the van to narrowly miss a giant tractor that was bumbling along, dragging a vast red machine behind it. The van's wheels skidded along aside a deep threatening ditch on her side of the road, before rejoining the road and continuing. Not for the first time on this journey, Daisy closed her eyes.

Shortly, they turned up a side road that narrowed into a bumpy track and Daisy looked up in amazement as the scruffy little van pulled up outside a most magnificent and imposing mansion.

"Welcome, to Le Guardian!" Dick announced, as he lifted her meagre belongings from the back of the van and led her up a grand set of steps to a gigantic front door.

The inside of the house was even grander than the outside, with high vaulted ceilings and splendid décor that wouldn't look out of place in a Home and Garden magazine. After a brief tour around, Oinky had been shown into a small stable within a courtyard at the rear of the house, and Daisy to a grand boudoir, off the massive landing at the top of a staircase wide enough to drive a tractor up it. The superfluously decorated bedroom even had its own bathroom, with an old fashioned type bath standing on little legs in the centre. After a couple of days trekking around the country, Daisy spoiled herself by talking a long and well-needed luxurious bath, filled with a sweet smelling concoction of bat-salts. Afterwards, wrapped in pale pink soft towelling dressing gown she inspected the room, admiring the view from its tall windows of the fabulous rolling countryside. She really had fallen on her feet this time, thought the girl, stifling a long yawn. When she bounced backwards on to the bed, it was as soft as a thousand tons of goose feathers and within minutes she fell fast asleep with bright smile on her face.

Daisy was not sure how long she had been asleep or, at first, even where she was, as she woke with a start. Outside, the sun was dropping behind a distant hillside, smothering the sky in a blanket of burgundy as it ended its long day. On the dresser beside the window, her jeans and t-shirt were washed and neatly folded in a smart pile. Hurriedly, she pulled them on, and headed downstairs, following a delicious smell towards a door off the hallway.

"Good evening, my dear!" smiled Dick, who was now wearing a dark-green apron and fussing behind a similarly dark green shiny stove. "How are you with black radish?" Daisy didn't know how she was with black radish, as she ran her hands through her spiky hair with a confused look on her face.

"Thanks," she said, sleepily, "for doing my laundry."

"What, that, oh think nothing of it. Quick wash and spin, no effort at all. And..?"

"And?"

"Black radish..?" he quizzed again, indicating to something pale and slightly fragrant in the pan on the hob.

"Oh, fine, I'll eat anything."

"Marvellous. It's not everyone's cup of tea," he added. "Oh, my dear, tea! How awfully rude of me, would you care for some?" He waved his hand vaguely across towards another part of the enormous kitchen. "There's a fresh pot over there."

Daisy made her way to the other side of the room, stepping over a sleeping dog which barely registered her movement. Removing a white and red spotted cosy, she poured herself a steaming cup of tea from the china teapot.

"Do want some?" she called to Dick, above the noise of the sizzling pan.

"Non, Merci," he replied, indicating to a half empty glass of red wine on the counter next to the hob, "I am having a little aperitif. It is after six o'clock, so it is allowed." Instinctively, Daisy glanced around for a kitchen clock and saw the time, 8.45. She had been asleep for over 3 hours. As she turned back to the man, he was producing a string of pink sausages from the fridge and she instantly thought of Oinky.

"I had better go and feed the pig!"

"All taken care of, Daisy," replied Dick, raising a sharp knife and severing the sausages from each other. He smiled a crooked smile towards her. "All taken care of!"

The girl headed towards the door, a little more hurriedly than she intended.

"Just going for some fresh air," she muttered.

"Well, don't go far, dinner in five minutes. In the dining room."

Daisy raced down the long corridor, trying to remember the way out to the back courtyard. Something about Dick had suddenly cast a doubt in her mind. She tried three doors, until she eventually found the right one, and jumped down the steps, still in her bare feet, onto the paved yard. When she reached Oinky's door, she looked over it, fearful of a strange inner feeling that it may be empty. Fortunately, her worries were overcome, as the pig lay there, sleeping like a baby, next to an empty feed bucket.

With a sigh of relief, she told herself to stop being so silly. Dick was a nice man, he wouldn't harm him, would he? Negotiating her way back across the yard, she went back into the big house and retraced her steps back to the hallway, looking for the dining room. All the large glossy doors looked the same, it would take her a while to remember which one was which. She tried one, turning the brass knob and pushing it open as its hinges let out a mild creak of resistance. Behind the door was a beautiful sitting room, adorned with peculiar works of art on the cream walls. Although this wasn't the room she was looking for, Daisy found herself drawn inside, the cold parquet floor slippery under her bare feet. She studied the pictures, one at a time, trying to make out what they were of. Modern art had never been her choice, she had never understood it, but some of these were beautiful, if only by their own ugliness. At one end of the room was a sofa, big enough to sleep a couple of people, and yet its grand dimensions were not out of context, such was the scale of this room. It was made of soft brown leather and she couldn't resist sitting in it, to test it out. As she sat down, a couple of sheaths of paper dislodged from the arm and fluttered down to the floor. Daisy reached down and picked them up, the writing on one of them catching her eye.

Dick Pyle enjoyed cooking. He was a man who considered himself creative, and the kitchen was somewhere he could express himself in his own domain. Cooking also gave him chance to think. He considered the Irish girl and her pet pig. She seemed a nice enough sort of kid, if not a bit naïve, and he didn't mind looking after her for a few days. Heaven knows, if she was able enough, he may even find some work for her, he could always do with an extra pair of hands around the farm and it was nice to have a bit of company. But it wasn't really her that he was interested in, kindness and pity to a stranger wasn't the real reason he had invited her back to the house. It was that pig. When the time was right, he would have to make the girl a sensible offer to buy it, so that the pig was rightfully his. He didn't want to steal it, if he could help it.

A loud beeping noise from the oven's timer alerted him that the vegetables were cooked, dragging his thoughts back to the kitchen once more. Dick turned off the oven and then retrieved the steaming sausages from the pan.

Meanwhile, in the sitting room, amongst the comfort of the gigantic leather sofa, Daisy was reading a document she had accidentally picked up from the floor. It was an invitation addressed to **David and Maidie, Edinburgh,** and it said:

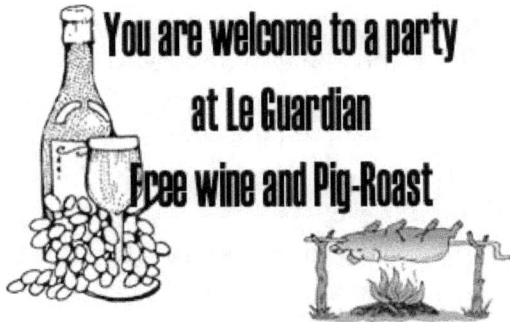

You are welcome to a party
at Le Guardian
Free wine and Pig-Roast

The invitation was for a date the following week. 'Pig Roast?' Daisy shuddered when she saw the picture. Was that why he had invited them back to this house? Before she had chance to get ever more paranoid, the door to the sitting-room opened.

"Oh, there you are! What are you doing in here? This is my private room. You are not to come in here, do you understand?" reproached a rather irate man with a plate of pork sausages in his hand.

23

Daisy tried to block out the sound of the cockerel crowing outside her window. In fact, it was so loud, that at first she thought it was inside the room, but then she remembered that she had left the bedroom window open last night as it had been so warm. Pulling a pillow tight up around her head, she refused to open her eyes to let the daylight blight her cosy sleep. She had thought she heard some other sounds too, out in the courtyard, footsteps and other muffled animal noises, as she drifted off back to her deep sleep.

* * * * *

It took quite a few hours to carry all the wood to build the bonfire, with teams of men, women and children all silently helping out with the task. Some of the men and women she recognised, that boy with the earring for one. And that one looked just like her Mother over there, only older. Eventually, His Lordship said that was enough and they could rest, flicking his wrist towards the fire. Instantly, flames crackled through the dry wood, giving off a bright glow into the dark sky above.

"Bring on the sacrifice!" he sang, the notes tuneful and crystal clear. Two men in police uniform carried a large black sack and set it down on the table before the Lord.

"Your Lordship, we deliver to you, this worthless animal, so that it may be sacrificed in the name of the hallowed Truffle."

"All hail, the hallowed Truffle!" chanted the group of helpers, rhythmically, who were now all wearing white robes. Daisy was wearing one, too. The powerful Lord slowly unzipped the bag to reveal a small wriggling pink creature, which looked helplessly up at him with pathetic eyes.

"Hallowed Truffle! We present a PORK sacrifice to you, so that we may all be forgiven for our unworldly sins!" The Lord's words sang out again, this time in the tune to a pop-song Daisy had heard before as, somewhere behind him, a backing band played along with the melody. The man raised a deadly silver knife above the small creature, as the band played louder, drums rolling as the fire raged higher. Except, Lord Pyle was now no longer a man, because he had the head of a giant mushroom.

"Oiiiinnnkkkk!" screamed Oinky.

"Nooooooo!!" screamed Daisy, as the blade slashed down...

*   *   *   *   *

Daisy woke with a jump, breathing heavily as cold sweat ran down her back and soaked the cotton sheets. A dream, it had been a dream. Her eyes focussed on the room around her. Yes, that was it. She was staying with this man. This was her room. She reached up and ran her fingers against the mahogany headboard of the bed and over the silky cotton pillowcase. This was real. That had been a horrible dream.

Unsteadily, she climbed from the bed and padded over to the window in her bare feet. Outside, the courtyard was quiet except for a few chickens scratching around one dusty corner. Low in the distant sky, a mottled haze of orange and yellow signified that the sun was rising from its sound night's sleep, ready to work another day's magic in the name of nature. From this window, the girl could see to the far end of the yard, where Oinky would be in his stable.

"Oinky," she called out in a loud whisper. It was the sort of whisper that one uses to check if another person is asleep, but hoping not to wake them if they are. "Oinky, are you awake?" There was no sound.

Daisy let out a long yawn, politely covering her mouth with the back of her hand and blinking her watering eyes at the clock beside the bed. 6.30am. Another hours sleep wouldn't hurt, would it? Outside, the air felt damp, almost chilly, and she closed the window to shut it out. Yawning again, Daisy crawled back under the covers and pulled the welcoming warmth tightly around her.

* * * * *

Oinky Grub looked up from underneath his straw bed at the man peering over the door at him.

"Oink!" he said, sleepily, considering it was far too early in the morning to be woken. The man opened his stable door and stepped inside, causing Oinky to jump up, looking for a better place to hide.

"Shhhh!" whispered the tall man, "I've brought you some breakfast."

This was more the sort of noise that Oinky liked to hear in the early morning, and he went to greet the incomer, inquisitively. Sniffing the air, his little brain recognised this person, it was Mr Tasty-mushroom Man.

Mr Tasty-mushroom Man put a handful of barley into his wooden trough and waited. Oinky was just scoffing the last of it up, when the man reached down and quietly clipped a lead onto Oinky's collar.

"Come on, little fella, we are going for a ride."

Oinky wasn't sure he wanted to go for a ride, and started to squeal but the man quickly produced something from his pocket that muffled the squeal instantly. It was a tiny piece of tasty-mushroom.

At 6am, Oinky followed Dick Pyle out through the yard gates and, with a little more encouragement of the mushroom variety, into the back of the small white van. The van was parked on a slope and Dick let off the brake, freewheeling down towards the road, before starting the engine, so it couldn't be heard from the house. Oinky wasn't too sure about this, and oinked his disapproval when the engine burst into life and the vehicle sped off down the road.

The evening before, while the girl had been sleeping, he had paid the pig a visit, to give it a closer inspection. His initial observation had been confirmed when, from ten paces outside its stable door, he had held up a small black truffle. From lying in near silence, the pig had gone almost demented within seconds, oinking loudly and scratching at the door to get at the object.

In all his years with truffles, he had used dogs to seek them out. It is a fact that truffles are very hard to locate, as they mainly grow just below the surface of the ground, around the roots of oak trees. Since he had been in France, Dick had owned two dogs, and he had trained them, to some degree of success, to seek out truffles using their good sense of smell. His truffle hounds, he had called them. But then one of them had been poorly and, over the last few years, Penny had required more and more medication for internal problems and not been much use for work. Sadly, she had died earlier that year, almost breaking Dick's heart, as he buried her in the garden and planted daffodils on her grave. His other dog, Valeta, had not been the same since, constantly pining for her lifelong friend. And his business had not been quite the same, either, as his truffle hunting exploits had been less and less fruitful. A few weeks earlier, he had been considering getting another dog, and was discussing with a close friend about which sort of hound was best for sniffing out truffles.

"Why not get a pig?" Christelle had said, jokingly, "they have great truffle noses." After that, he hadn't really given the idea much thought. That was until yesterday afternoon, when fate had delivered one to him, on a plate, so to speak!

Not just any pig either, but one with such an exceptional sense of smell, that it could detect a truffle from at least ten paces. With a bit of training, this animal could become a very useful asset indeed. He already had illusions of not only finding hidden truffles in amongst his own oak trees, but of heading out into the wild forests and seeking out hordes of them from beneath some of those ancient old oaks. Local folklore spoke of giant growths of truffles in the Pyrenees area, but nobody had ever managed to uncover them.

The van slowed down and pulled to a halt outside a pair of padlocked gates.

"Come, little piggy, let's see what you can do?" said Dick, as he opened the rear door of the little van.

Oinky had not enjoyed their early morning drive through the lanes. In the back of the small white van, the floor had been very slippery and as they rounded each corner, Oinky had been bowled around like the numbered balls in a lottery tank. Now, as the vehicle had stopped, he felt quite sick and needed some fresh air.

"Come on, little piggy," said the voice again, throwing the doors wide. Oinky came on. He came on at great speed; out through the open door, on to the damp grass and squeezing under the padlocked gate. He did all this rather fast, much faster that Dick's early morning reactions could cope with.

"Come back here, you stupid creature!" called out the man in anguish. He fumbled in his pocket for the keys, opened the gate and then sprinted after the small pig, as it made its way down the rows of trees. "Come back here, aw, come on. Please!" Then he tried another approach, softening his tone.

"Come on, Oinky piggy, look grub!" Dick pulled out his pocket knife and cut up a small piece of truffle.

It had been quite a long time since young Oinky had run free in an open field. In fact, it had been so long ago that he barely remembered his mother and his siblings at all. But he could vaguely remember a few things. Acorns, for instance, he had eaten them through the fence. And here he was now, in a field, with the sun rising over the trees, racing around free, where the floor was littered with acorns. Oinky stopped running and snuffled down on the ground, crunching up the tasty morsels, three at a time. This was more like it, he didn't feel quite so sick any more.

"Come on, little piggy, come here little piggy," called a voice some way behind him in the distance. Oinky focussed on the figure of Tasty-Mushroom man waving something in the air. What he saw was the man take a small object from his pocket and open it up. Now Oinky was not an expert in many things, but one thing he could recognise, even from a hundred paces, was a knife. Yes, the last time he had run free in a field, a man had chased him with a knife. That man had caught him too. Oinky instinctively looked round at the place where his tail would have been, had that man not caught him on that day, and then he bolted down through the rows of trees, as fast as his legs would go.

After nearly two hours of searching, Dick Pyle, completely out of breath and ideas, gave up his fruitless search amongst the oak tree plantation and dejectedly plodded back up the field towards his white van. Once or twice he had caught sight of the pink creature, but as soon as he had crept up on it, the thing had spotted him and disappeared again. It was hopeless. In this plantation, there were nearly a thousand trees and, down towards the bottom, was a massive undergrowth of trees and brambles that even the hardiest dog would have trouble penetrating. That was where he had last sighted Oinky, and that had been half an hour ago.

Dick quietly pulled the small van back into the yard at Le Guardian and shuffled into the house, his legs aching from hip to toe. There was no movement from upstairs, as he flipped on the kettle, and he didn't think the girl had woken yet. Good. Now, he had to think up a story and his mind was racing with ideas.

How would they catch the pig? Well, he had a reasonable idea about that one. If they couldn't coax it out of the wood, he knew people in that business who could deal with it.

What would he tell the girl? That was more of a problem; the thing had been her pet and he didn't think she would be too amused if she found out he had been coveting it for business purposes. She would be even less amused when he told her he had lost it!

He pulled a couple of rashers of bacon from a pack in the fridge and tossed them into the pan, which he put on the hob and lit the gas. Then, dropping down into his favourite armchair by the warm oven, Dick reached for the phone and dialled a number from memory.

"Christelle, my dear, I hope I didn't wake you?...No? Good," said the man in perfect French. "Pardon? There is a bit of *crackling* on the line." He shook the phone and put it back to his ear, raising his voice louder above the static on the phone-line and the noise of sizzling bacon. First in French, and then again in English, he shouted the words: "I got that pig...!"

Awakened by the noise of the van returning, Daisy had got dressed and was just about to open the kitchen door, when she heard the voice shouting from inside.

24

A look of sheer horror spread across Daisy's face as she pulled open the unlocked door to the empty stable. Like a tramp rummaging in rubbish bins, she searched through the deep straw in a vain hope that Oinky may still be here, hiding away under the straw, sleeping. But he wasn't and, in her heart of hearts, she knew he wouldn't be.

"I got that pig!" The words went round and round in her mind, as the smell of cooked bacon wafted out from the house like the smell of, well, the smell of cooked pig, I suppose. Daisy felt nauseous....for a while. And then she felt extremely angry, as she strode purposely towards the house.

"What have you done with him?" Her green eyes were narrow, hiding the fire behind them, as she calmly asked Dick the question, like a police officer interrogating a witness. Dick was equally calm, as he sat and ate his bacon sandwich in the armchair.

"Hmmm?" he muttered, with his mouth full.

"Oinky? What have you done with him?" The smell of the bacon was making her feel sick again. "He's not there. Where is he?"

"Oinky?"

"Yes. My pig. You know perfectly well what I am talking about!" Her voice was rising of its own accord. "Where have you put him?"

Dick's face stayed dead pan, not rising to the provocation, avoiding Daisy's accusing eye contact. Inside he was thinking fast, as the denial arrived on his lips.

162

"I have no idea what you are talking about. I assure you, he was fine when I last saw him." There, that wasn't entirely a lie, was it? He waited patiently while she repeated her accusations again, before delivering the line that would certify his innocence.

"Was the door locked?"

Daisy stopped in her tracks, eyeing the man as he raised his eyebrows questioningly. Was the door locked? No, the door wasn't locked, but that was no defence, was it?

"No," she said, finally. "No, it wasn't locked."

"Really?" Calmly he placed the empty plate down on the sideboard next to his chair, chewing the remainder of the sandwich before continuing. "Not locked, eh? Tell me, did you visit your pet last night, after I had given it food?"

Daisy knew the answer to this, but she also knew she had closed the door firmly after her. Something about the way Dick referred to Oinky as 'IT' fuelled her suspicions. She thought before answering, knowing this would be the end of this interrogation. For now anyway.

"Yes," she said eventually. "But I am sure it was locked then."

Dick's face turned to a more friendly smile, as he raised himself up from the chair, his knees creaking as they complained bitterly about the overuse they had endured that morning. Daisy instinctively backed away, despite his re-assuring manner.

"Well, it seems your pig may have escaped, my dear. Maybe you didn't lock the door firmly enough, and now he's broken out?" The man opened the fridge, retrieving the pack of bacon and peeling off a couple of rashers. "Would you care for some breakfast?"

Daisy fled from the room, tears welling up in her eyes. The old man had been right of course. Oinky could have pushed the door open and escaped. But she was pretty sure she had fastened it up, the evening before. Then she thought back to the words she had heard, when Dick was on the telephone. "I got that pig!"

Out in the yard again, the young Irish girl started calling out her pet's name, as she looked through the shadows. "Oinky, Oinky, are you here?"

Oinky couldn't hear her calls, of course, but he could hear other sounds in the dark wood around him. He lay shivering for quite a while, buried beneath a thicket of green bracken and brambles as he listened to the scary sounds. He had watched the Tasty-mushroom-with-knife man walk back up the field, some while ago, but he still waited patiently until he was sure the coast was clear. All the while, the sound of distant wild animals closed in nearby. Leaves on the bushes around him started to rustle, as he listened to approaching footsteps. The reason the leaves rustled was because he was shaking so much; shaking with terror. Then a twig snapped and so did his brain. With a frightened oinking, the small pig jumped to his feet and bounded out in the open ground again, not daring to look back.

For a while, Oinky wandered aimlessly along the rows of young oak trees, eating a few acorns and considering the situation. Here he was, out in the open air at last, a pig with freedom, and plenty of food. This was the life. He should be safe here, as long as he kept away from that scary woodland. But he did miss the girl, a tiny bit. She had been kind to him, except when she had made him wear those ridiculous clothes. But now she had delivered him to this man who chased him with a knife. Oh well. Oinky was just about to lie down and get some sleep, when a powerful odour emerged, just at the far reach of his senses. It was a smell that he recognised. Letting his nose do the work,

164

Oinky effortlessly tracked the smell to a nearby small tree and then down to the ground by its roots.

I am not sure how familiar you are with the ways of the porcine species, but you may wish to know this fact. Something that they are blessed with, besides their exceptional sense of smell, is the ability to dig up earth, not with their feet as some lesser creatures do, but with their nose.

Nobody started a stopwatch! Indeed, there was no official timer recording how long it took Oinky to unearth that truffle, but let's just say it was pretty fast. If discovering truffles, digging them up, and then eating them was an Olympic event, then meet Oinky, newly crowned world champion Tri-athlete! Or should that be tru-ufflete? When the clock stopped (supposing it had been started), there was no ceremony, nobody to cheer and hand out gold medals. But Oinky didn't need a medal. Oinky had his own reward, thank you very much; tasty-mushroom for breakfast. Tasty-mushroom, right there, in the ground under a tree? And Oinky was in a field of approximately one thousand of trees!

Meanwhile, Daisy's searching had not been so fruitful. Dick had come out to help her, and suggesting that she check out in the fields, but Daisy was still suspicious of him. The way he kept producing bacon and sausages, and the fact that he was inviting friends round for a pig-roast, was never far from her mind. The statement: "I got that pig!" she deduced, was him bragging to one of his friends that he had captured the essential ingredient that is required for a pig-roast. But what had he done with him? Daisy tried not to think about it and she definitely tried not to cry. But the more she tried not to do either of these actions, the more she did. Floods of tears clouded her vision as she wandered down the narrow lane, trying hard to call out the pig's name through her sobs until, eventually, she found an old tree-stump and sat down and let the tears flow.

The Irish girl had always considered herself a good judge of character, someone who could spot a good person from a bad one. And, usually, she was someone who was able to deal with both. But how had she been so wrong about Dick Pyle? He seemed such a nice man. Would he do this to her? Could a nice man just take her pet, and then…? She couldn't bring herself to think the word…kill.

The poor girl's mind didn't know which emotion to lead with. Should she be in rage? Should she be desperately sad? Optimistic? Panicked? Revengeful, even? As she sat on the tree-stump, as confused as a Parisian tourist, her eyes did some work of their own and, from what they saw, a little more clarity arrived. Because what they saw, at the base of that gnarly old tree-stump, were some mushrooms growing in an untidy clump. Wiping the tears away, she inspected the clump more closely, with their brown and red caps, decaying with age. She picked one, and held it to her nose, and was just considering tasting it, when a voice behind her caused her nearly die of fright.

"Pas manger, Mademoiselle. C'est par bon!"

"Jeez, you nearly caused me to die of fright!" she shouted, as though she had read the last paragraph. "What the devil do you think you are doing, sneaking up on me like that?" She said a few other words as well, things that she may have heard her mother say, many years before, but thankfully no one else heard them.

"Pardon, Mademoiselle, je suis desole," replied the voice, which belonged to a young man, his dark featured face appearing out from above the hedge. Daisy jumped to her feet, embarrassingly trying to wipe the tears from her cheeks, as she turned to face him.

166

"What are you doing, spying on me like that?!" Her cheeks flushed red and her confused emotions supplied her with an assortment of rage and panic, in equal measures.

"Ah, you are engleesh?"

"No, I am not," replied Daisy, wearily. It wasn't worth explaining that Irish was not English, not to foreigners anyway.

"What do you want?" she said again, sharper this time as she stamped her foot. The young man cocked his head on to one side, a smile spreading across his face like jam on a tea-cake.

"I do not like to see a lady, cry. It is not good!" Daisy's mind wanted to say, "Well go away then, and stop spying on me!" It wanted to be angry at him, but something in that smile was as infectious as a baby's giggle, and Daisy felt her own mouth joining in, despite her sadness and anger. For the first time, she looked into his blue eyes, registering the kindness that lay behind them. But then, another part of her mind, the bit that was still quite angry with the rest of it, suggested that she wasn't as good judge of character as she thought she was, and warned her to be careful.

"What do you want?" she asked again, wiping the smile away. Bustling his way through the narrow hedge, he appeared before her, all six feet of him. Daisy tried her hardest not to notice how handsome he was but it wasn't easy.

"Pierre," he said, still smiling at her, and then bending down to sniff the piece of mushroom she had been holding. "C'est poison!" he said, his dark eyebrows lowering into a frown.

"I thought it may be a truffle?"

"Truffle? Ha, no such luck. Truffles do not grow on the side of the road!" Pierre smiled again. "Now, please sit down and tell me why you cry?" Daisy's conscience still wanted to tell the stranger to mind his own business, as her body obediently sat back on the old tree-stump.

"I lost my pig!" she announced, glaring at him in case he was about to laugh. But something about this Pierre told her that he wouldn't laugh at her, his eyes were the listening kind.

So she told him how she had just arrived with her pet, and about Dick Pyle. Pierre nodded knowingly when he heard Dick's name mentioned so she carried on. The pig had gone missing this morning, but she had fears that Dick may have taken it… Her eyes started to well up, but she managed to get the word out this time. Dick might have killed it, for his pig-roast next week! Pierre interrupted at this point by raising his hand, seeing the girl's distress, and climbed to his feet. Again Daisy's mind rang an alarm siren through her head like that of a lost ship on a foggy night, but she was powerless to resist, as he put a comforting arm around her.

"Your pig will be fine. You'll see!"

The man had been right in that respect; her pig couldn't have been finer, for he was fine dining al-fresco, in an open-air French restaurant, on a delicacy worth approximately three thousand pounds per kilogram! And he had been for some considerable time.

Dick, on the other hand, was not fine. Not fine at all. For he now had a problem on his hands. The girl had suspected him, but that wasn't the problem. With enough persuasion, he could probably throw her off the scent. No, she wasn't the problem at all. Yesterday, he had discovered an animal that could make him money and now, before he had chance to use it, he had lost it again. They needed to track it down and capture it, quickly. Christelle had offered the services of her hunting hounds. They were used to tracking wild boar, so a small pig would be no problem. But there had been one stipulation, as Dick gave her the coordinates of the pig's last sighting. The pig was not to be harmed!

If Dick had any idea as to what 'the pig' was doing at that precise moment, he may have reconsidered this decision.

It wasn't too long before Daisy, and her new-found handsome friend, heard the angry cries of rabid boar-hounds in the near distance. They weren't the only ones to hear them, either. Oinky stopped feasting and listened to the fearful din, before bolting down towards the dense wood. Now, he had a decision to make, and Oinky wasn't very good with decisions. To go into the scary wood, or to stay out here near the even scarier angry cry's. Frying-pan or fire? It wasn't easy. With exuberant fear like that, coupled with a rather indulgent meal of truffles and acorns, Oinky was quite unable to contain a less than healthy smell that radiated out behind him as he ran!

Unfortunately, it was a scent that even the weakest nosed hound would be able to follow. And believe you me, these hounds had noses that could lock onto that smell like a radar-guided rocket-missile! Four huge dogs with flapping ears and razor-sharp teeth gained on the trufflete, like sports-cars in a bicycle race.

"Le *chasse!*" said Pierre, hurriedly, "come on, I can help you!" Daisy and Pierre ran along the narrow lane, towards the sound of the hounds, her legs struggling to keep up with the big athletic chap, as he barely broke a sweat. As they neared the top of a steady incline, a red pickup truck was parked in a gateway, indicating the place where the hounds had been unloaded. Daisy heard them, giving tongue, the noise eerily echoing back to her from a forest in the distance.

Then she heard that she was desperately hoping not to hear. A piercing squeal!

*   *   *   *   *

Dick was apprehensively pacing the kitchen in his tattered carpet slippers, awaiting a phone call from Christelle. Despite his anticipation, when it did ring it still made him jump.

"Ca va?" he blurted out into the receiver.

"Non," replied the caller. "I think they have caught the pig, in the woods. It doesn't sound good!"

"Didn't we agree that the animal wouldn't be harmed?" When the answer came back to him, he held the phone away from his ear. Christelle replied in rapid French, about how difficult it was to stop four excited hounds that were used to savagely ripping their prey apart, limb by limb.

Dick felt the heat rise under his collar. Perhaps, in hind sight, this hadn't been such a good idea. He only hoped it had been quick. Now what would he tell the poor girl? It would be unfair of him to report back to her that her pig had not only escaped, but had been eaten. And what about his truffle enterprise? That pig was going to be his salvation.

"OK," he instructed, at last, "make sure they don't leave any evidence!"

"Oui." The line went dead.

Dead, and buried. That was the end of this saga, then.

25

Pierre sprinted down between the rows of young oak trees, following the loathsome sound of four hounds, with Daisy some way behind him. When he neared the thick coppice of the wood, the sounds had quietened to a muffled chomping noise. Christelle was standing there at the edge of the thicket, calling her animals. Pierre stopped, and the two French people looked each other in the eye.

"C'est fin?" he asked. The woman gave a shrug, her eyebrows raised.

"Oui. C'est fin." It's finished.

Pierre turned away. He was a man who had grown up with hunting, as had his father and his father before that. He was a country-man from rural surroundings. But even he, a hardened farmer's son, could never quite get used to the way hounds killed their prey; chasing the animal through the roughest terrain, and then dragging them down by a hind leg.

Daisy arrived by his side and he didn't have the heart to look her in the eye. She looked at the Christelle, who was now whistling for her hounds to return…..and screamed.

*

At this point you, the reader, may be somewhat upset. You may also be wondering why the story should end up this way and, indeed, why it has run to another chapter. Well….

* * * * *

Deep in the dark wood, a small herd of wild boar stopped running, the eldest one checking around and counting their numbers. They were one short. The missing one had been elderly and, quite possibly, nearing the end of its life, anyway.

In an entirely different part of the same wood, a small creature heard a sound that it recognised. The sound it heard, was Daisy's scream, as it squeezed itself deeper into a hollowed out tree trunk.

"Oink," it said. Then it waited. And it listened.

Oinky had heard Daisy's cries, way in the distance, and had heard the sound of the rabid dogs, as they were carted away. Eventually he heard, nothing. So he slept.

For what the large hounds had failed to expect was that they were not just tracking a small pig without a tail, but an experienced racing pig. Oinky had run faster than any pig had ever run before, so fast in fact, that the hounds he had distanced himself enough from the hounds that they had picked up a different trail, that of a small pack of wild boar.

When he woke, it was still quiet outside the tree trunk apart from the rustling of a few trees above him. Oinky had no idea where he was, as he managed to squeeze himself out from the hole. Although he had been terrified after the chase, it had somehow gained him a little more confidence, knowing he could out-run some fairly experienced hunters. He wondered amongst the towering old trees, looking up to the sparkling light way overhead, where they all seemed to be holding hands. Up in the branches, birds and squirrels flitted about, not taking much notice of him, as he rooted about among the dead leaves for acorns. In a small clearing, there was a clump of yellow flowers, and Oinky sniffed them before biting off their heads. He remembered flowers, about the time when he had been in a garden and devoured a whole patch of them. But then a man had chased him, with a knife! Men often did that.

While he was mooching innocently in the undergrowth, his nose picked up the scent of what had now become his favourite food, some way in the distance. Oinky slowly followed the smell that eventually brought him to the foot of the biggest tree he had ever seen. The great oak tree stood in its own clearing like a sentinel, barging the other trees out of its reach. Its girth was so wide, it took Oinky a good few minutes to walk all the way around it, in fact he kept walking a few times, somewhat disorientated about where he had started off from. But definitely, in one part, the smell of tasty-mushroom was at his strongest, and that is where he started to dig. As he dug, routing up the stubborn earth with his twisted snout, the smell got even stronger, almost over-powering.

"Oink!" said Oinky, in excitement, quietly at first, and repeatedly louder. The more he dug, the more he became oblivious to the world around him. Here was a trufflete on a mission.

Except, the more he oinked, the more the rest of the forest took notice of him. Within minutes, animals started closing in. One of those animals only had two legs. He also had two barrels.

＊　＊　＊　＊　＊

Daisy was a girl who had grown up through the school of hard knocks. When things got her down, she was never one to revel in misery, she always tried to bounce back. As she trudged back up the field towards the road,

174

with Pierre's big comforting arm around her, she tried to console herself that it was only a pig. Pigs get killed and eaten every day, don't they? It wasn't even her pig, not technically, just one she happened to have made an acquaintance of, so to speak.

"What will you do now?" asked the boy, as if reading her thoughts.

"Me? Oh, I dunno, probably drift on somewhere else," she sighed, brushing the last of the tears from her sore eyes. "I am not going to stay with that man, anymore. Murderer that he is!"

"He didn't do any murdering…?"

"Well, he as good as did. It must have been him who let the pig out of the stable. I am sure I didn't do it."

"Maybe it wasn't your pig?"

"What?" Daisy stopped.

"Maybe, it wasn't your pig. Down there, in the woods?"

"It's a bit of a coincidence, isn't it? My pig goes missing, then a pig gets caught by hounds."

"I have friends, I will make some phone calls. OK?"

"Don't bother. He's gone. I have to get over it!" Tears started to well up in Daisy's eyes again. Pierre squeezed his arm a little tighter around her, then stopped and turned her round to face him. He really did have nice eyes and a most charming smile.

"Maybe..?" He stopped and looked away.

"Maybe, what?"

"It's OK. I do not think I can ask."

"Ask what?" She returned his smile. The boy was blushing slightly when he took a deep breath and looked into her green eyes again.

"Maybe, you could come and stay with me?"

For the first time in her life, Daisy felt her heart jump into her head, tugging her emotions together into a huddle, like a crowd of team players discussing tactics before a game. It caught her completely by surprise and instantly she pulled herself away from his grasp. He said nothing, just standing there, gazing at her, this gawkish man. This great handsome chap; strong enough to take on the world but yet looking so helpless, waited innocently for her answer, as though he was on a train platform checking the timetable.

The battle raged in Daisy's conscience. Never trust a stranger. Don't do it. Don't look into those smouldering, gorgeous eyes. You don't need his comfort, you can defend your own battles. You don't know anything about him. STOP. Think....!

"OK," said the part of her brain over which she had zero control, "if you have a spare room."

"C'est parfait!" he replied, his relief spreading to yet another smile, as he put his arm around her once again, and continued heading up the field.

When they reached the gate, Pierre pulled out a mobile phone and dialled a number, speaking in rapid French that Daisy was unable to understand. After the brief call, he spoke to her again, using his excellent English.

"That is all settled. You go back to Le Guardian and collect your things. I will go back to the farm and then come and fetch you in a few minutes. I just spoke to my brother, who is out in the woods today."

Daisy stood and watched him go, rooted to the spot as her mind raced back over what had just happened. What was that feeling that had come over her? She had never felt anything remotely like it before.

She crept in through the courtyard to the back-door at Le Guardian, and was about to knock. On the walk back, Daisy had been considering what to say to Dick Pyle. She had no proof of anything. The man had been kind enough to her and taken her in. Maybe he wasn't to blame? Perhaps it had been her fault all along. She went to knock on the door, but then thought better of it and turned the knob quietly instead, hurrying silently through the hall and up the stairs. Quietly, she gathered her few possessions into her small bag and crept out again, without saying goodbye.

In the kitchen, Dick let out a sigh of relief as he heard the back-door click close.

26

Pierre Rouchet had never experienced anything like it either. It was as though a whirlwind had blown in though the front door of his brain, scattered chaos and confusion everywhere, and then left without explanation. At sixteen, he had always lived with his parents on their small farm and had worked hard. On weekends he played rugby for the junior team at Toulouse and had turned out to be quite good at it. He was used to hard work, and tough physical contact, as they trained 3 evenings per week. Despite his good looks, Pierre had never really found time for girls. Not until today.

When he arrived back at the farmhouse, his mother was just about to quiz him about this stranger who he had invited to stay with them, when his mobile phone rang.

"Oui, Jermone. Ca va? Oui? C'est fantastic!" When the phone call ended, his mother started her questions again. Who is this girl, where did you meet her? Pierre dismissed her enquiries with the flick of a hand.

"Just make up the spare room and an extra place for dinner," he told her. "I have to go." And with that he hurried to the barn, flinging the door open and grabbing something he needed from a pile by the door, before jumping on to his scooter. The ragged machine spluttered and coughed as he kicked down the lever again and again, muttering words of encouragement. Eventually the ancient old two wheeler burst into life, releasing a cloud of thick exhaust into the barn. Pierre revved the engine and sped off down the lane, heading towards the bottom end of the deep woods, where his brother had just phoned him from.

Expertly, Pierre manoeuvred the bike along the grassy track, avoiding the deep ruts and pot-holes, as the back wheel scratted for grip. The motor-scooter had belonged to his grand-father, who had passed away a few years back, and the boy had sort of inherited it, after his older brother had used it for a year. In France, you are allowed to ride a scooter on the road at 16 and this clapped out machine was his only mode of transport. It was called Edith. His grandfather had named it after Edith Piaff, the great singer.

Edith's engine laboured, making quite a din as it roared into the entrance of the forest. It wasn't the only thing making quite a din either. A small creature had been minding its own business, as it happily dug up the earth under a big tree in search of tasty mushrooms, until it looked up into the two barrels of a shotgun. Behind the gun was a young man, who was talking to him in a foreign language. He couldn't understand what the man was saying but, as it happens, it loosely translated into: 'Say your prayer's, piggy!' Oinky was frozen to the spot, as the man started to squeeze the trigger. This was surely the end. Cat's are rumoured to have nine lives. Pig's on the other hand, have quite a few less than that, and this little creature had pretty well used most of his up. With calm abandon, Oinky awaited his fate, as he stared up barrels of the loaded gun.

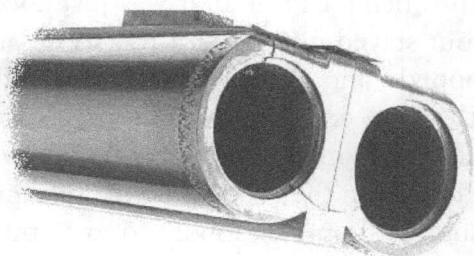

And then, in what is possibly the biggest coincidence in this story so far, somewhere in the deep recesses of the man's pocket, a telephone had rung. For the split second that the man's concentration was distracted, the little pig spotted his chance and took off, oinking and squealing very loudly indeed.

The phone call had been from a man called Jerome, brother of Pierre, who was not very far away. It had said something like, 'keep an eye out for a small pig, and if you see it, capture it, alive! There is a reward.' Something like that anyway.

So, keen to grab the reward money, our nameless hunter put down his weapon and chased after Oinky, tracking him through the thick undergrowth. In a gallant attempt to hide, Oinky had found his way back to the safety of his hollowed out tree-truck.

By the time Pierre arrived at the scene on Edith, two men were guarding the hollow log, one at either end, while Oinky lay shivering inside, frightened and oinking.

Some more hurried French conversation happened, followed by a long stick being poked up one end of the hollow log. The stick reached Oinky, prodding him with the sharp end as Oinky looked forward down the tubular hollow. Oinky wasn't too keen on being prodded by sticks but, compared to being captured, it was just about bearable. He squealed, but stayed put. After a few more attempts, the prodding stopped and there was more conversation, combined with some scratching of heads, as his would-be captors considered other methods of extracting our shivering trufflete from the security of his safe-house. Other methods included shouting loudly down the one end, banging on the roof with rocks and attempting to lift up one end to tip him out. The latter method was doomed to failure, as the trunk weighed in excess of one ton, even without a pig in it. Like a seasoned anti-war protester, Oinky was not to being moved. If it was a game of chess, this would be considered stalemate.

"Maybe they should wait until it was hungry?" suggested one of the hunters. This was then discussed at some length, until Pierre came up with a rather natty idea. Under guidance from the other hunter, the boy negotiated his way back to the giant oak-tree, leaving the other two guarding the pig-in-the-poke. After considerable effort, Pierre managed to continue digging where the pig had already started, and uncovered a substantial growth of black truffles. Making sure nobody was watching him, he carefully removed all of them, brushing them down with his hands, before hiding the stash in a nook of the tree where he would later be able to come back and retrieve them, and sell them for a substantial profit. Then he broke off a tiny piece and took it back to the hollow tree-trunk, much to the appreciation of the other two men.

The rest was easy, really.

A sack that Pierre had brought from the barn was positioned at one end, with the truffle in it, and time pretty much did the rest. Within ten minutes, the animal's will-power had given way and Oinky was now contained in a hessian sack, roped on to the luggage-rack of Edith, as Pierre raced along the road and up towards Le Guardian leaving a trail of black exhaust and squeal behind it.

Inevitably, Pierre met his beloved Daisy walking in the other direction. He stopped and they embraced. Then she climbed on to the back of the already over-laden scooter and the three of them headed back to the farmhouse for tea and cakes.

* * * * *

If this book were a fairytale, that would have been a reasonably fitting ending to it. Unless, of course, they all ate the pig for supper? Which they didn't.

But it isn't a fairytale, it's a piggytale, and a piggytale deserves to be told in full. So...

27

George Ryan didn't really enjoy watching rugby. It was a game that he had neither played nor understood, and it seemed dastardly rough. But the chaps at the golf club watched it religiously, and it was always a topic that was keenly discussed on most Monday mornings in the office. With that in mind, and the family being out shopping, George settled himself in front of his new TV on a rainy Saturday afternoon. George was proud of his new TV; it was top of the range. He scanned the channels again. Today some French side were playing against his local team, London Harlequins, so he flipped it on and listened to two men in a studio, confusingly discussing rucks and mauls, as well a the finer points of box-kicks and decoy-running. All these baffling terms were alien to him, but he did his best to keep up.

Just as the game was about to begin, he heard a car pull up on the driveway. That would Donna and Sarah arriving back from their shopping trip to disturb his peace. Hopefully they would stay in the other room.

After much fanfare, on the giant TV screen, the two teams emerged on to the pitch. The articulate commentator was lamenting about how French rugby sides often bring a cockerel with them as a team mascot. The French were big on mascots, it seemed. But this side from Toulouse had gone one step further with their mascot this year, and brought with them…..a pig.

* * * * *

At first Oinky had been a little scared of all the huge mean looking rugby players, with their scary faces and shovel-like hands. Some of them were as tall as pine trees and one man had so many scars he looked like he had been in a plane-crash. But, for all their anger and rough-and-tumble on the rugby pitch, most of the men were very gentle with Oinky.

With Daisy's permission, Pierre had volunteered Oinky to be mascot for the Toulouse team, which meant that he got to go with them on the team bus every weekend. He quite liked going on the bus as the players used to feed him biscuits throughout the journey. Some days he would get to run around with them too, as they used him in their training sessions. After all, a player who could catch a racing-pig at full tilt would be a useful match for any opposition. Not that they could catch him though, but Oinky had fun letting them try.

And so it was, that the Toulouse rugby team had set off to play an away fixture in a far away country. It had been a long journey, although Oinky had slept for most of it on the back seat of the luxury coach, occasionally sitting up to look out of the window.

He wasn't so sure about this big field with the short grass though. When the players had all run out, he had joined them, as crowds cheers and music blared. Oinky ran around the pitch looking up at the thousands of faces, as well as taking the occasional bite of grass. After a few minutes, the crowd settled down and a short man with a whistle took up position in the centre. Oinky eyed him with suspicion. The man looked across at him, and pointed to the exit. Oinking look at the exit and then took another bite of grass. The crowds laughed. Then the man jogged over to

Oinky, but Oinky jogged away. The man pointed to him again, this time blowing his whistle.

Thirty rather large rugby players, all dressed in brightly coloured shirts, heard the whistle and assumed, quite naturally, that it was to signal the start of the game. One man kicked the ball in the air and then everyone started running everywhere. Another man caught it, and then twenty nine people jumped on him. Oinky watched them from somewhere near the twenty-two metre line.

Again, the referee blew his whistle, but this time a couple of the men who had been lying on the floor started swinging punches at each other. From then, things got out of hand. The watching throng of spectators cheered on the brawl, which soon involved most of both teams, drowning out the sound of a whistle being blown by an irate man, who was getting red in the cheeks. Oinky backed away slightly, until order was restored. Some medical-looking people ran on to the pitch to mop the blood off the man who had started the fight, while the other two teams glared at each other from ten paces.

Meanwhile, the referee had a word with their captains, demanding them to behave, to stop fighting and also to, please, remove what appears to be a small pig from the try-line. A couple of men in blue shirts set to the task, as instructed, running at Oinky with their arms out wide. Oinky watched them cautiously.

"Oink," he said to himself, just as they were approaching, and headed swiftly down to the other end of the pitch at a gallop, as three men attempted to tackle him. This raised a huge cheer from the watching audience, as well as much laughter.

* * * * *

George Ryan watched this with interest. Nobody at work had ever mentioned animals competing in any games? This rugby certainly was a mystifying sport? To his amazement, he watched as both teams, three match officials, two sports coaches and a few medical staff all chased a small pig around the hallowed turf of The Stoop stadium in West London. It certainly was entertaining, and he couldn't wait to join in Monday morning's discussion on the subject. The sitting room door burst open.

"Daddy, look what we bought, look what we bought!" squealed George's daughter, as she bounded into the room waving a bright red pair of shoes. George glanced at them briefly, smiled to the girl, and then turned his eyes back to the proceedings on TV.

Sarah Ryan suddenly lost interest in the new shoes too, as her eyes locked on to the TV screen.

As the commentators did their best to give an accurate account of the situation, two girl's voices, which were approximately 125 miles apart, shouted out the same two words, simultaneously.

"Oinky…GRUB!"

A slender girl with spiky hair sauntered on to the pitch, waving a small morsel in the air, calling out the words again. Oinky, who for once was quite enjoying being chased, didn't actually hear the voice calling, above the noise of the encouraging crowd of spectators. But, as he ran past the penalty spot for the third time, his nose caught a whiff of his favourite food. Tasty mushroom.

"Oinky…GRUB!?" The words sunk in and the pig screeched to a halt. Well, he would have screeched, were he on tarmac, but instead it was more of a slide. Followed by some more sliding. And even more sliding, followed by

186

some squealing, as approximately forty bodies landed on top of one small pig.

By this point, George was up out of his chair, cheering and clapping, despite being completely baffled about the rules of the game.

Somewhere amongst the pile of bodies, a referee's whistle was blowing profusely. Daisy walked up to the assembled steaming muddy heap.

"Oinky...GRUB!?"

A small dirty pink face poked out from under the belly of an overweight prop-forward, shook its ears, and then wriggled its body free.

"Oink?" it said.

And there it was, the whole amazing adventure, told in full.

Except, you probably want to know what happened next, don't you?

Well let's just say, as in all good piggytales, everything worked out reasonably well in the end.......

Daisy May went on to marry her French man and they started a pig farm in Gascony with the money they made from selling the largest clump of truffles ever recorded. She changed her mane to Florette.

Pat MacGowan sold his pig-racing business and returned to Dublin, where he hooked up with a singer he had once known. They now do a double act, with Pat playing along on the fiddle.

Ricky Warner, another rogue who had literally been on-the-fiddle, ended up in prison for selling illegal alcohol.

Dick Pyle still runs his successful truffle business and now has a team of well trained pigs working for him. And he never did hold that pig-roast. You should look him up at

www.truffle-tree.com

Barry Edwards became a powerful businessman by the time he was twenty, while his father, predictably, went out of business as the price of pork declined.

Officer Tabelle went on to become chief of police, and thankfully he never encountered another disturbance by a small pig on the streets of Paris.

Soon afterwards, **Stellios the Greek**, disappeared without trace.

Maximus eventually grew too fat to run, and ended up....well, it's best not to think about that.

George Ryan never did get into rugby and took up watching table-tennis instead.

Sarah Ryan? Well Sarah went on to be a successful theatrical agent, with only one client.

So it all ended alright, really.

THE END

Who?
What's that you say?

Oh, him? I nearly forgot.
Well....

28....

That really is the end of the story, except to say that Oinky went on to be a very famous pig and had a happy life.

After he was spotted on TV, he was commissioned to make adverts for a well know biscuit manufacturer, one who made cream-crackers. From there he got into the film business and even had his own luxury home built, where he frequently dined on tasty mushrooms.

But in order to do this, he needed a good agent to look after him.

And fortunately, he found one called Sarah Ryan.

THE END
(again!)

Have you read Andy's novels about Princess the cow?

Titles in the series are:

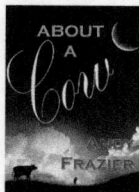

Book 1 - **About a cow**

Princess is a young half-breed calf who grows up through hardship and bullying on a farm in Scotland. When her best friend dies her life gets set on a mission towards one destiny, the Great Royal Show. By pure chance she meets someone capable of helping her fulfill that dream.

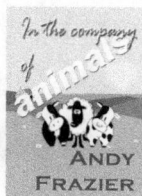

Book 2 - **In the company of animals**

Having been sold to a man who rents animals out for money, Princess is kept in prison-like conditions. She meets some new pals and they form a lasting friendship as they plan their escape and a bid for freedom.

Book 3 – Cow Factor

Princess has always strived for fame and stardom and her big chance comes when she her and her pals get chance to compete on a TV talent show. But not everyone wants her to win.

Book 4 – The Royal Detective

Princess and her pals get a part as extras in a film about a Prince who is kidnapped. But during the film one of her friends disappears and Princess and her trusty sergeant become detectives themselves as they set off to find their friend a solve a mystery.

Other stories from Andy Frazier include:

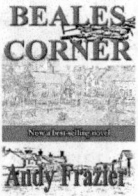

BEALES CORNER

Tom hears his granddad's stories but he doesn't really listen; his summer visits are just a break for himself, he has enough troubles of his own. When the old man asks him to help him record some of his memories he is not really interested; the past is in the past and that is where it should stay. If only it would..?

MOULIN

When Henry Harman's father buys an old windmill in France, he and his little brother think it might be a nice adventure. But up in the roof of the windmill lives an old owl that the locals refer to as the Protector. But what is he protecting and why won't any of the builders go inside the building. When Henry does manage to get up into the roof, he discovers an ancient diary written by a boy 850 years earlier. The boy says he knows a secret, one so dangerous that he dare not write it down. As Henry and his brother decipher the code, things start to fall into place and they set out on an adventure of a lifetime. But can they get home again…?

About the author

Andy Frazier is an author of children's stories. Occasionally he writes things for grown ups too, but he finds this quite hard as he has never quite grown up himself. He has always wanted to write, ever since he was a child, and now he can't think of anything he would rather do. He gets his most enjoyment out of creating colourful characters and then bringing them to life in humorous situations.

History

Born into a life of farming, it took a long time and a lot of determination to get away from it, but he thinks he has just about achieved that now. Andy did quite a few things during his career, including agricultural contracting, retail sales, sheep breeding and IT, before he somehow became a business analyst working in a city. Oh yes, and at one time he was an expert in grooming cows. It all made sense at the time.

One day, he had a eureka moment and upped sticks to South West France. He now lives there on a smallholding where he shares his time equally between his partner, some more sheep, some DIY tools and a set of golf clubs. Despite all the obvious distractions that renovating a big old farmhouse presents, Andy spends most of his mornings writing and that is the bit he enjoys most.

For more information, please visit
www.andyfrazier.co.uk

Please take a second to visit:

WELCOME TO
TRUFFLE TREE
IN THE HEART OF GASCONY

Adopt a Truffle Oak and gain not only the exciting possibility of your own truffles but also a piece of tranquil French woodland and an entrée to the cuisine, countryside and heritage of Le Gers.

www.truffle-tree.com

www.ingramcontent.com/pod-product-compliance
Lightning Source LLC
LaVergne TN
LVHW051631080426
835511LV00016B/2283